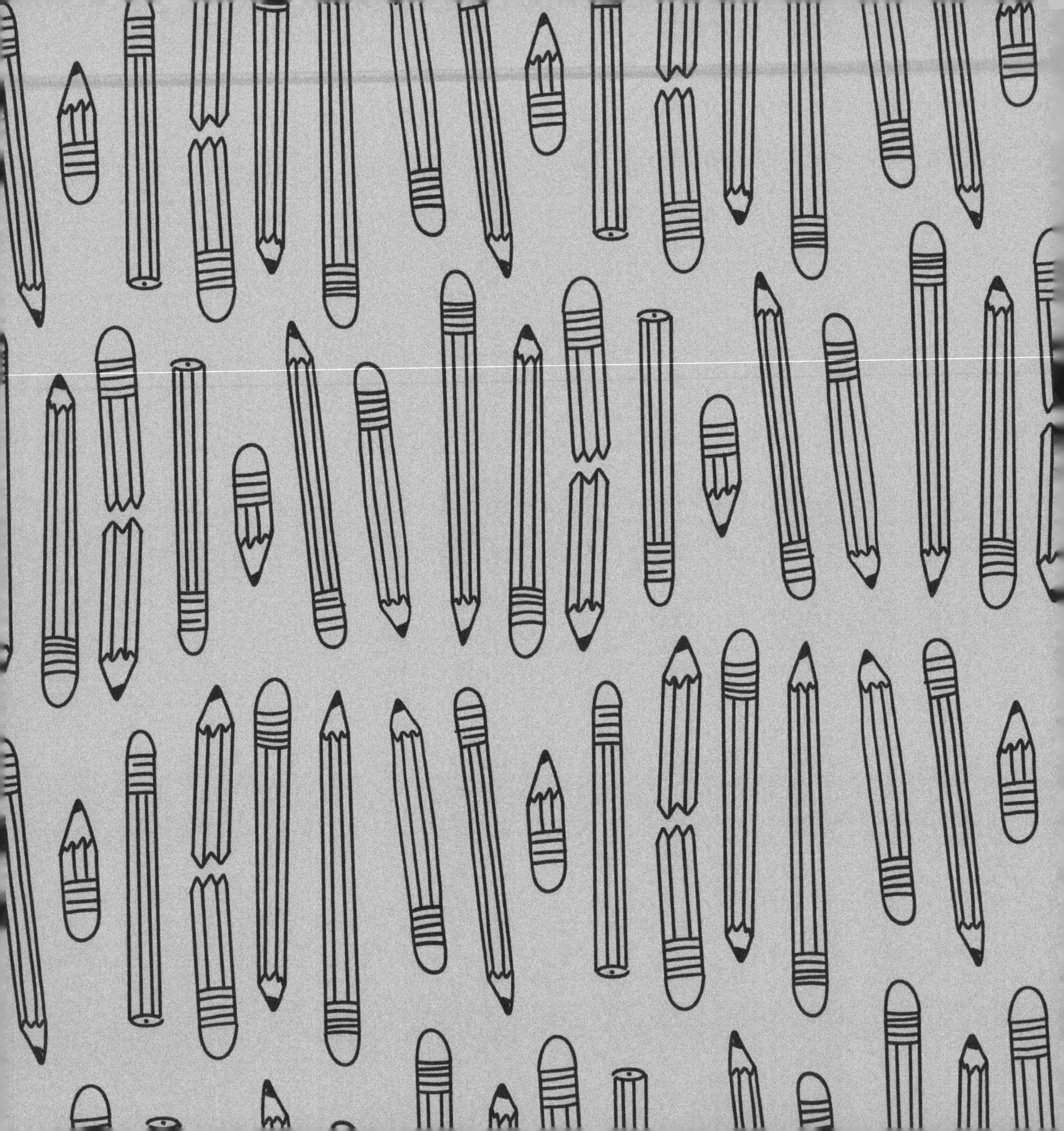

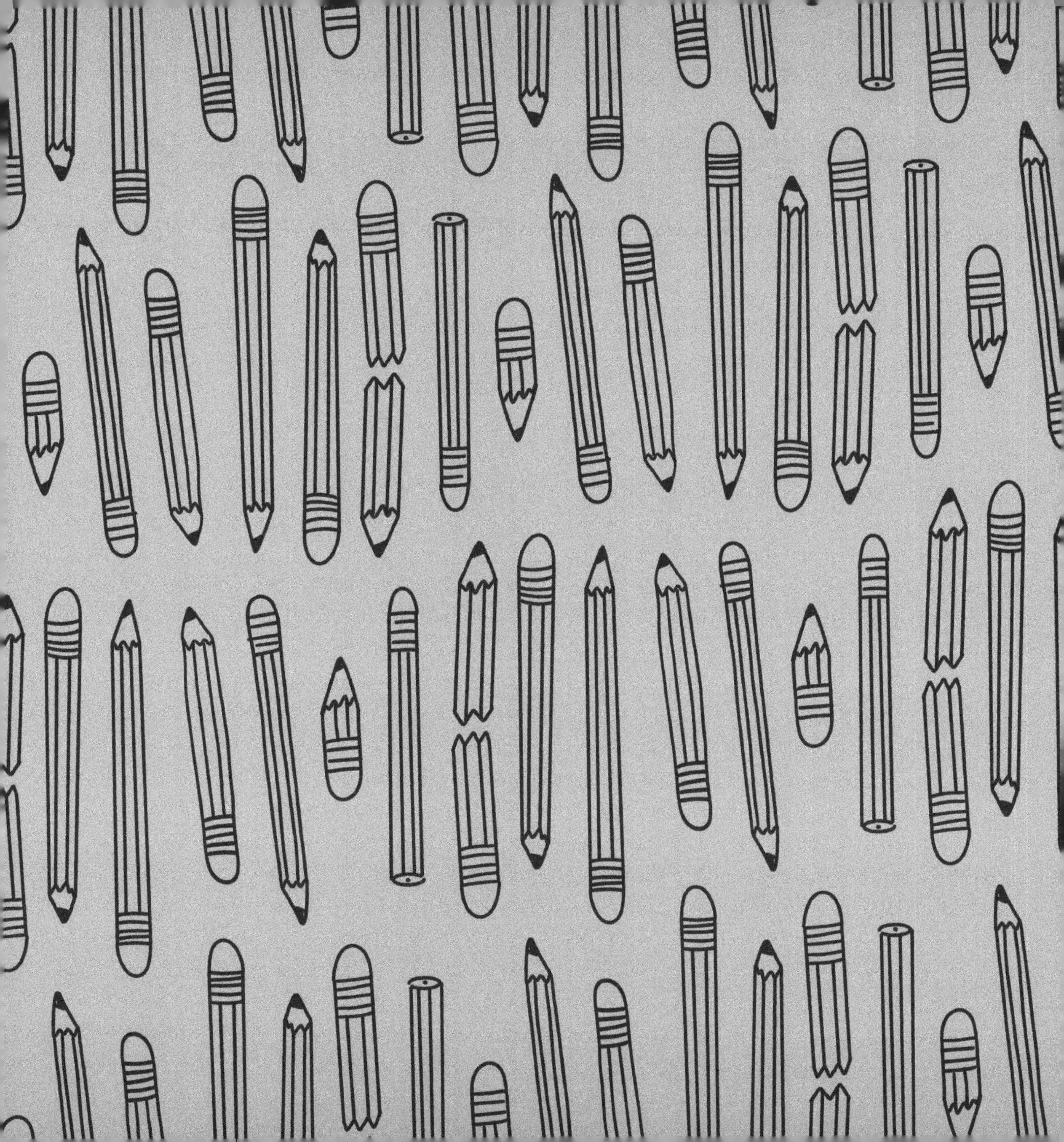

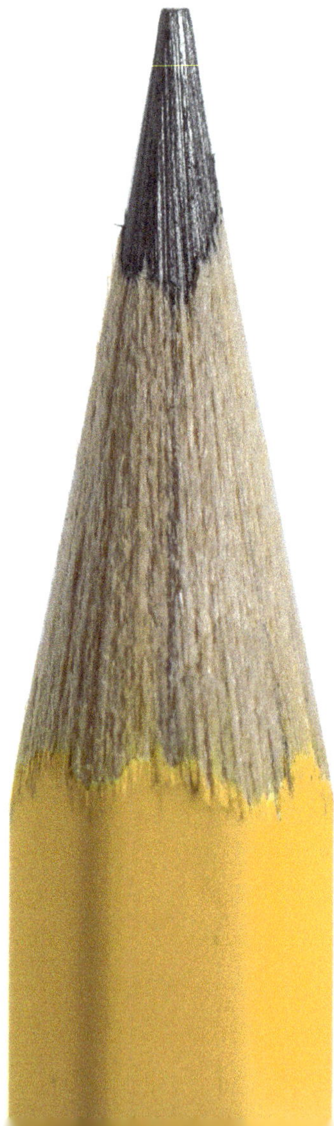

№ 2

Story of the Pencil

by William Allen

No. 2: Story of the Pencil

Editor: William Allen
Photography: William Allen
Photography: Musgrave Pencils/Emily Dorio
Illustrator: Jef Caine

Year of Publication: 2023

ISBN: 979-8-218-26079-8

Published by No. 2: Story of the Pencil, LLC
www.storyofthepencil.com

This book is dedicated to the **original creator** who unlocked humanity's ability to co-create the wood-cased pencil, and with deep gratitude to my wife **Jill** and our cherished children **Aubrey**, **Asher**, and **Amelia**.

In memory of Dr. Henry Petroski and Sean Malone.

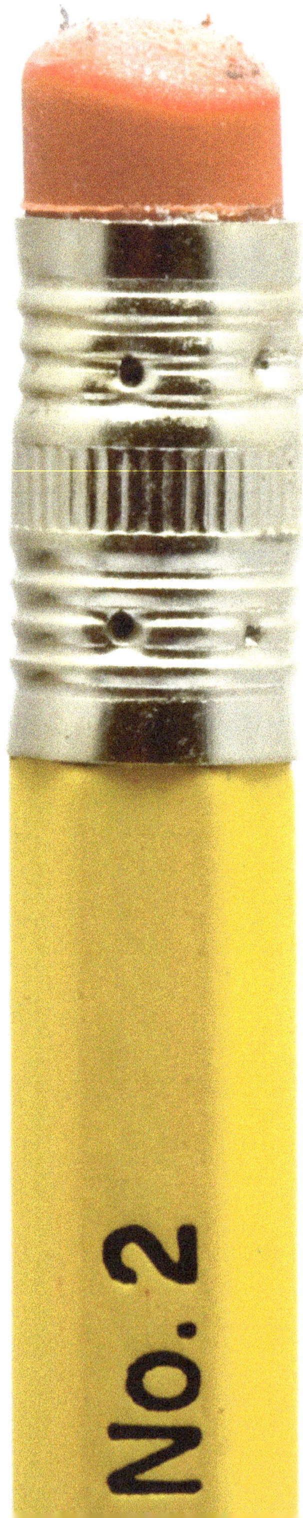
No. 2

Contents

Introduction by William Allen

In a world saturated with modern media and digital technology, the humble No. 2 pencil often goes unnoticed as a common tool. Yet, history tells a vastly different story. The Pencil, once a revolutionary invention, has shaped the course of human progress, leaving its mark on invention, craftsmanship, art, engineering, manufacturing, government, history, and business.

While the advent of digital technology has provided new ways to express thoughts and ideas, we find ourselves at a crucial crossroads. The significance of the pencil is at risk of fading into the background as society becomes increasingly reliant on binary code and screens. In this battle against time, we must ask ourselves: What will be lost if we abandon this analog piece of technology? How crucial is the pencil to human ingenuity and creativity? Should we care if it takes a backseat?

In pursuit of answers, I embarked on a global journey, seeking out the preeminent voices on the captivating story of the pencil. I connected with a diverse array of individuals, from the "poet laureate of technology" to an artisan pencil sharpener, media ecologist, pencil manufacturers, the "godfather of grunge design," designers, digital ethnographers, and more. Their insights and perspectives are woven into the fabric of this book.

Organized around four fundamental art principles - balance, distortion, emphasis, and value - the narrative follows a transcendental storytelling structure. As you delve into its pages, you'll find grid paper, encouraging you to sketch and write, in the hope that you'll rediscover the true significance of the pencil.

No. 2 is more than just an exploration of history; it is a charming and emotional tale of an ordinary tool that indeed changed everything. Through its pages, I seek to illuminate the profound and timeless impact of the pencil, inviting you to rediscover its magic and celebrate its enduring legacy.

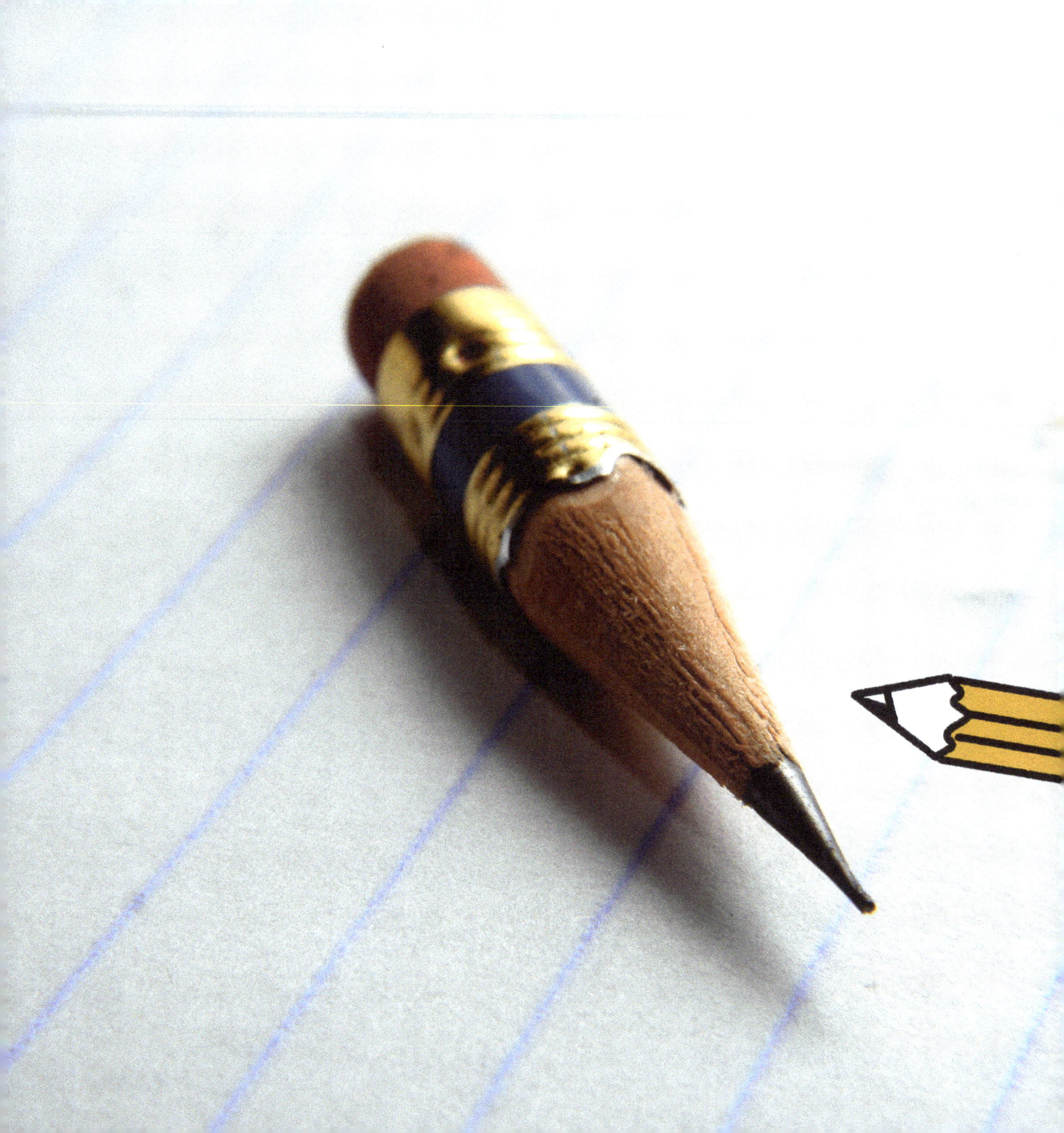

Balance

equilibrium achieved through thoughtful distribution of elements

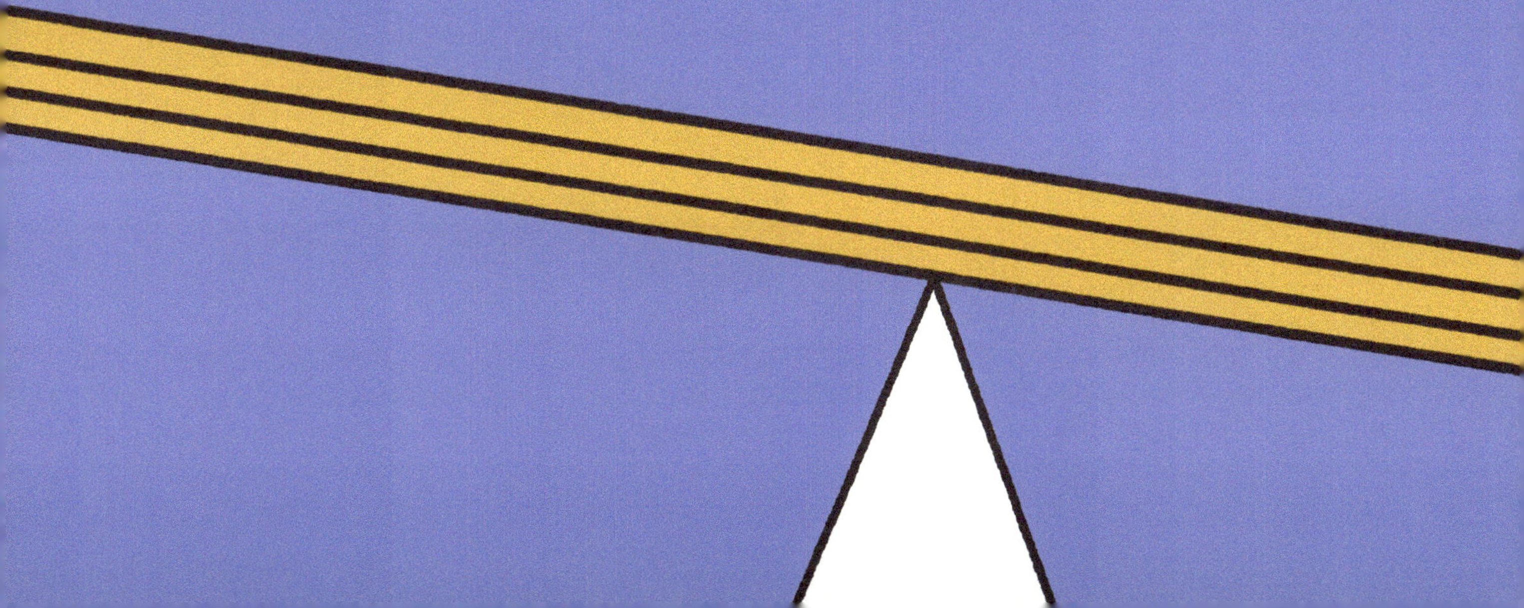

Coming of Age Story

Henry Petroski, Aleksandar S Vesic Professor of Civil Engineering and Professor of History, Duke University

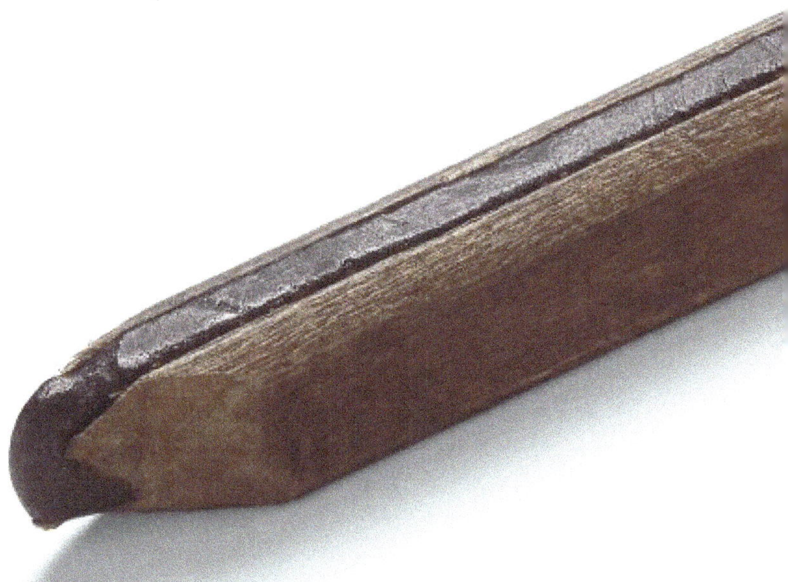

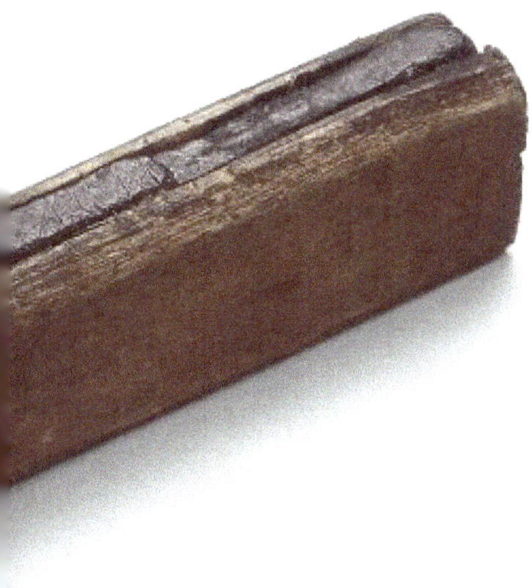

Early pencils were called "dry pencils." You don't need ink, you don't need watercolors, you don't need any wet medium. The pencil has a big advantage because you don't have to carry around a pot of ink, and maybe spill or lose it, or somehow have to hold it. The first discovery of a really good source of graphite was in the Lake District of England. It just came out of the ground, and you could write with it as is. Early people using this graphite to make marks started wrapping string around it, not to protect the graphite so much as to protect their fingers from touching the graphite directly. Eventually, they began to make grooves in pieces of wood, cut the graphite to fit those grooves—this would be pure graphite—and then cover up the graphite with another piece of wood, all fine, like cabinetry, and then those became pencils that were really the forerunners of what we know today as a wood-cased pencil.

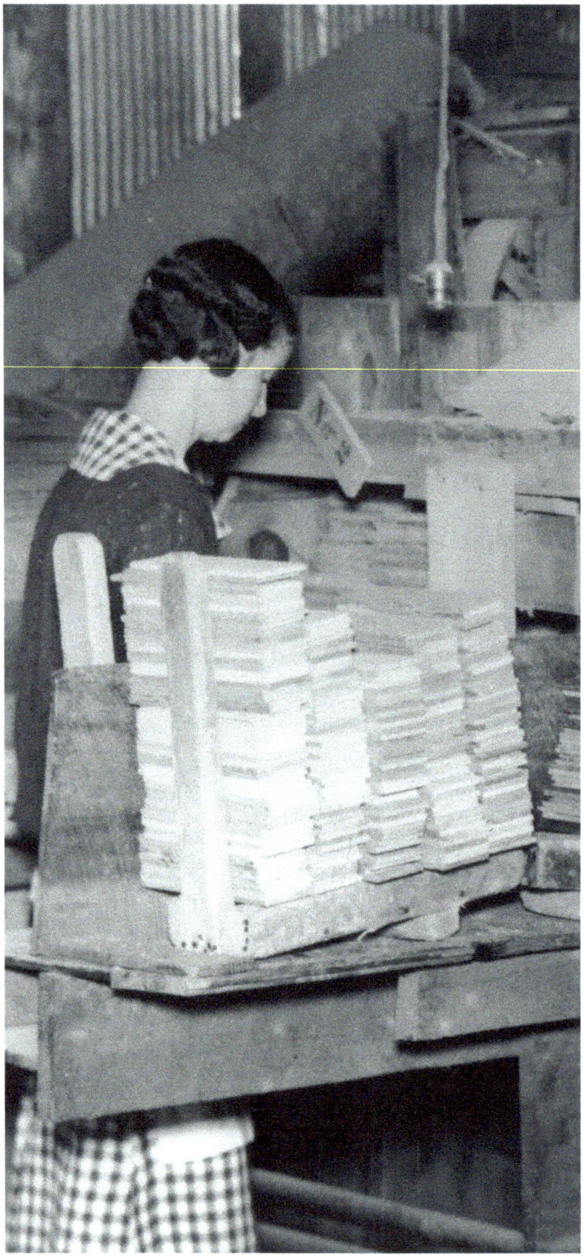

Wood

High-quality graphite was beginning to run out, but the process of refining it was improved. That problem was pretty much solved in making a lead-graphite combination. The wood is a different story. German pencil companies, back in the 1830s, '40s, and into the '50s even, knew the best pencil wood grew in Southeastern United States—Southern red cedar. But Southern red cedar was quickly exhausted. In fact, in the 1920s, pencil companies started buying up old barns or fences that were made of it, just to have a supply of wood.

Today, most of the pencils made in this country, and some abroad, use wood from the West Coast of the United States, called incense-cedar. It has a straight grain, so it's not going to warp, and it will hold the pencil lead properly. It will also sharpen without creating a lot of splinters. Who wants splinters when you're trying to write with a wooden pencil?

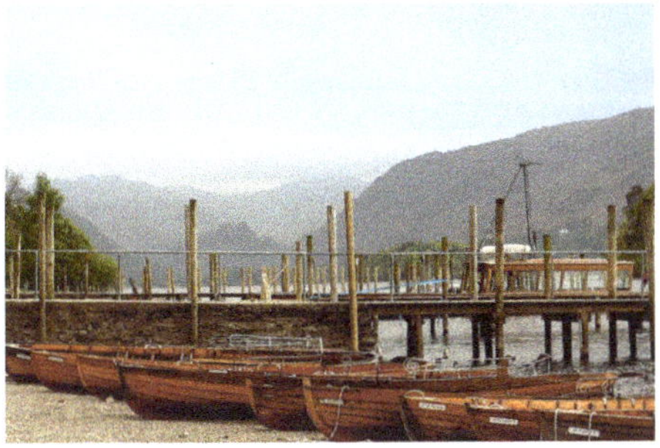

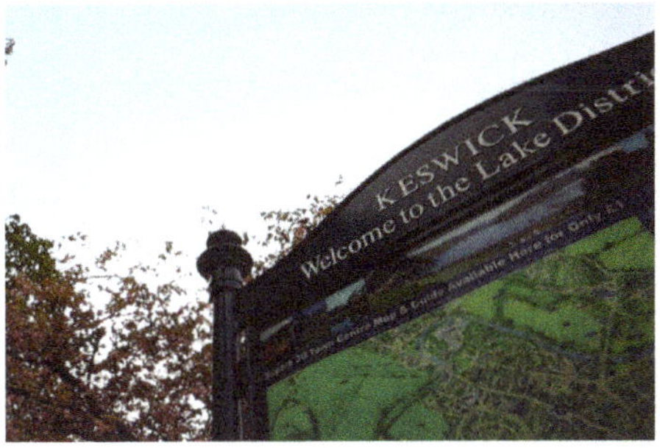

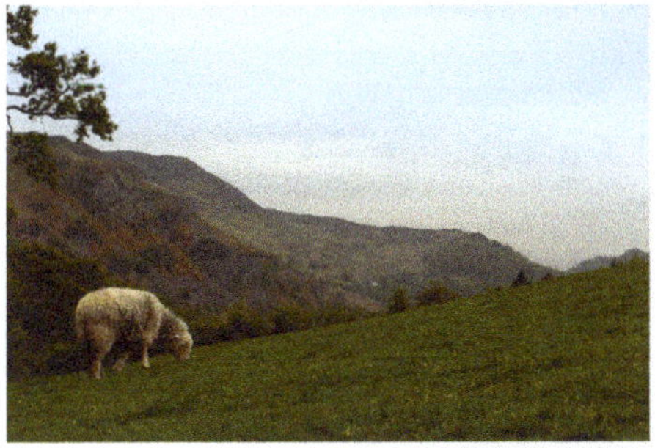

Lake District in England

Shape of the Pencil

Why is it hexagonal? Some historians say people who used pencils back then often wrote on sloped desks or drew on sloped desks. Therefore, everybody worried about their pencil rolling off the desk. However, one of the main reasons that large pencil companies made hexagonal pencils was because it was more economical. They could make about 10% more pencils out of the same amount of wood by making them hexagonal rather than circular.

Shade

No. 2 is sort of an average grade. It's not too hard, and it's not too soft. That means you're not going to press so hard to make a mark. At the same time, it's not going to wear out so fast. A happy medium.

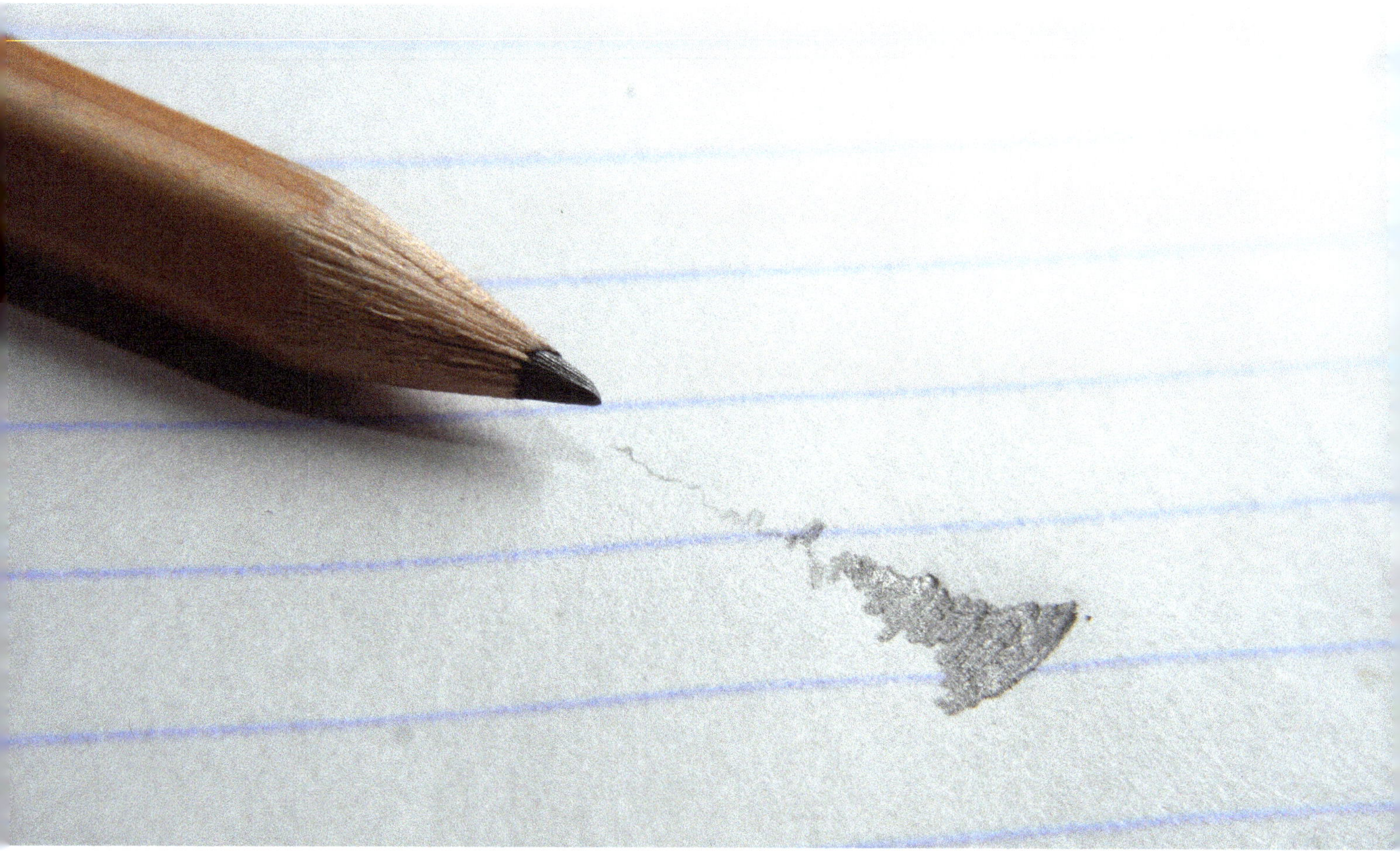

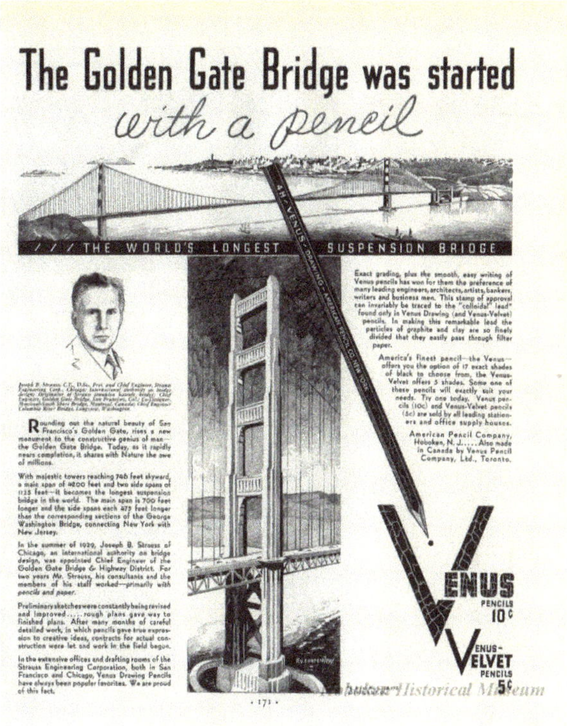

Pencil Ads

The idea of "Starting with a Pencil" is actually a theme from advertising campaigns by pencil factories back in the '30s. One in particular shows a picture of the Golden Gate Bridge drawn in pencil, and the caption was in big letters, saying, "It started with a pencil." Really, things like that do start with a pencil because they start with a concept, and then they get fleshed out. The pencil then comes into play again in the course of doing the calculations that are necessary to design a large bridge or a building. Therefore, the pencil really is central.

From an engineering perspective, old things and new things can coexist, and I think they often do. It's seldom that we're at work at a computer, whether it be a tablet or a laptop, or even a smartphone, that we don't wish sometimes that we have a pencil so we can jot something down, because we want to go to a different screen or something. Or, for whatever reason, we don't want to forget this URL, or we don't want to forget the numbers that we've just looked up. The old and the new can actually coexist happily together.

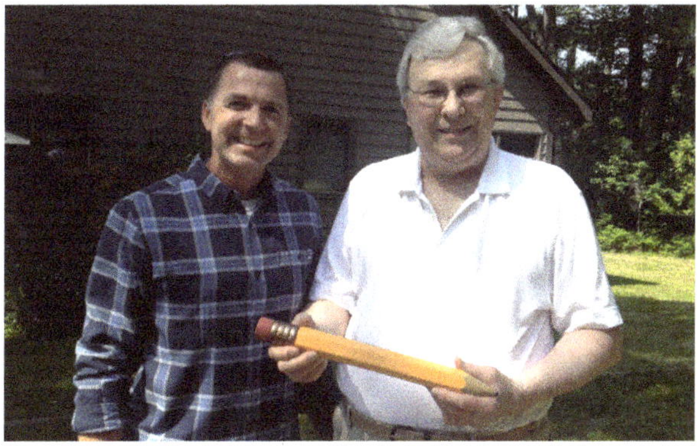

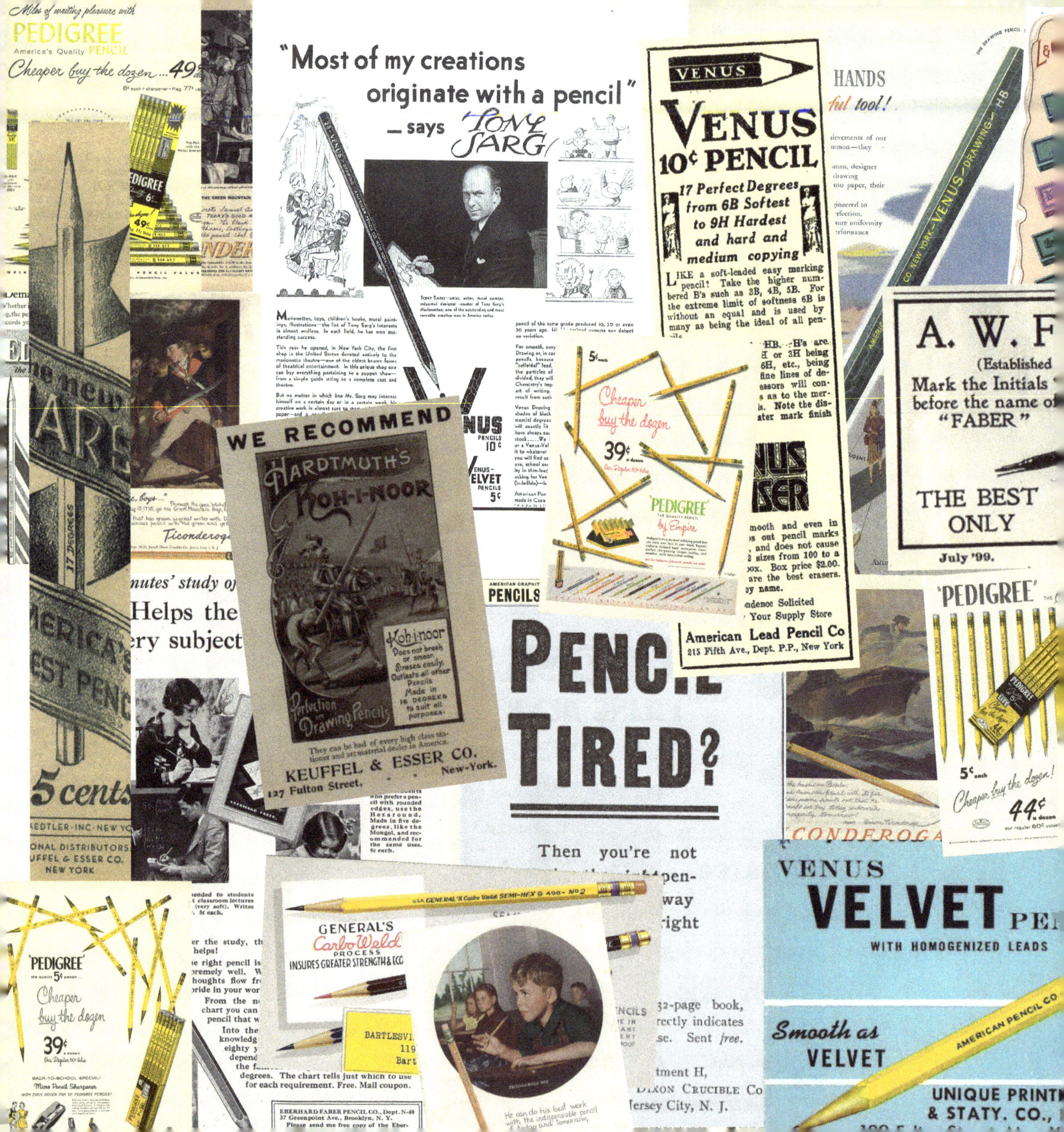
Miles of writing pleasure with
PEDIGREE
America's Quality PENCIL
Cheaper buy the dozen ... 49¢
"Most of my creations originate with a pencil" — says TONY SARG
VENUS
VENUS 10¢ PENCIL
17 Perfect Degrees from 6B Softest to 9H Hardest and hard and medium copying
LIKE a soft-leaded easy marking pencil? Take the higher numbered B's such as 3B, 4B, 5B. For the extreme limit of softness 6B is without an equal and is used by many as being the ideal of all pen-
American Lead Pencil Co
215 Fifth Ave., Dept. P.P., New York
HANDS
A. W. F
(Established
Mark the Initials before the name of "FABER"
THE BEST ONLY
July '99.
WE RECOMMEND
HARDTMUTH'S KOH-I-NOOR
Koh-i-noor Does not break or smear. Erases easily. Outlasts all other Pencils. Made in 17 DEGREES to suit all purposes.
Perfection in Drawing Pencils
They can be had of every high class stationer and art material dealer in America.
KEUFFEL & ESSER CO.
127 Fulton Street, New-York.
5¢ each
Cheaper buy the dozen
39¢ a dozen
PEDIGREE by Empire
PENCIL TIRED?
Then you're not
Helps the
ery subject
5 cents
AMERICA'S BEST PENCIL
Ticonderoga
GENERAL'S CarboWeld PROCESS INSURES GREATER STRENGTH & ECO
GENERAL'S CarboWeld SEMI-HEX 498 No 2
PEDIGREE
5¢ each
Cheaper buy the dozen!
44¢ a dozen
TICONDEROGA
VENUS VELVET PE
WITH HOMOGENIZED LEADS
Smooth as VELVET
AMERICAN PENCIL CO
UNIQUE PRINT & STATY. CO.,
DIXON CRUCIBLE Co
Jersey City, N. J.
EBERHARD FABER PENCIL CO., Dept. N-40
37 Greenpoint Ave., Brooklyn, N. Y.

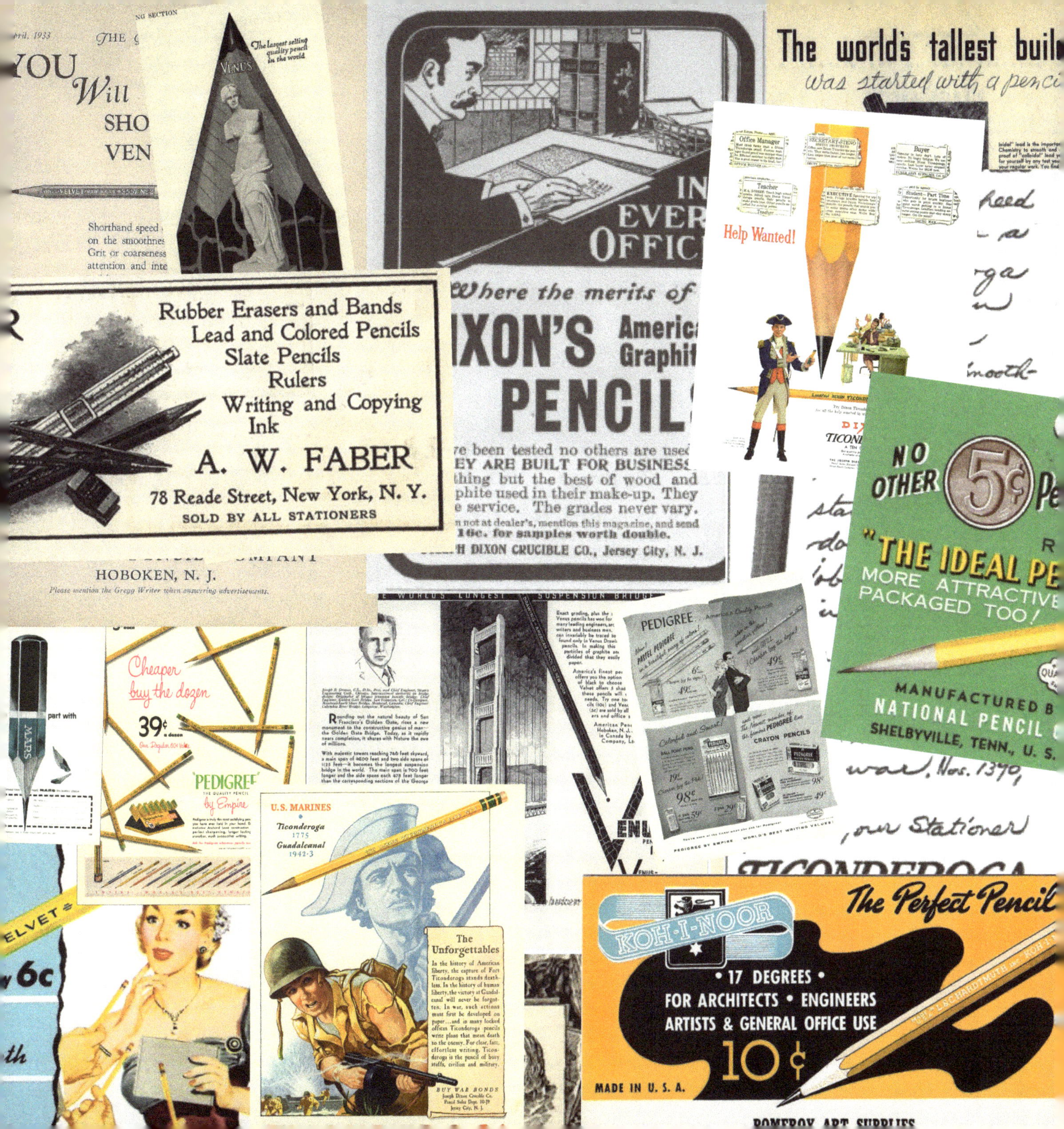

The largest selling quality pencil in the world
VENUS
Shorthand speed
Rubber Erasers and Bands
Lead and Colored Pencils
Slate Pencils
Rulers
Writing and Copying Ink
A. W. FABER
78 Reade Street, New York, N. Y.
SOLD BY ALL STATIONERS
HOBOKEN, N. J.
Please mention the Gregg Writer when answering advertisements.
Where the merits of
PENCILS
IXON'S
ve been tested no others are used
EY ARE BUILT FOR BUSINESS
16c. for samples worth double.
H DIXON CRUCIBLE CO., Jersey City, N. J.
The world's tallest buil
was started with a penci
Help Wanted!
Office Manager
Teacher
Buyer
Executive
NO OTHER 5¢
"THE IDEAL PE
MORE ATTRACTIVE PACKAGED TOO!
MANUFACTURED B
NATIONAL PENCIL
SHELBYVILLE, TENN., U. S.
part with
MARS
Cheaper buy the dozen
39¢ a dozen
PEDIGREE THE QUALITY PENCIL by Empire
PEDIGREE
CRAYON PENCILS
U.S. MARINES
Ticonderoga 1775
Guadalcanal 1942-3
The Unforgettables
In the history of American liberty, the capture of Fort Ticonderoga stands deathless. In the history of human liberty, the victory at Guadalcanal will never be forgotten. In war, such actions must first be developed on paper... and in many locked offices Ticonderoga pencils write plans that mean death to the enemy. For clear, fast, effortless writing, Ticonderoga is the pencil of busy staffs, civilian and military.
BUY WAR BONDS
Joseph Dixon Crucible Co.
Pencil Sales Dept. 10-J9
Jersey City, N. J.
ELVET
6c
KOH-I-NOOR
The Perfect Pencil
• 17 DEGREES •
FOR ARCHITECTS • ENGINEERS
ARTISTS & GENERAL OFFICE USE
10¢
MADE IN U. S. A.

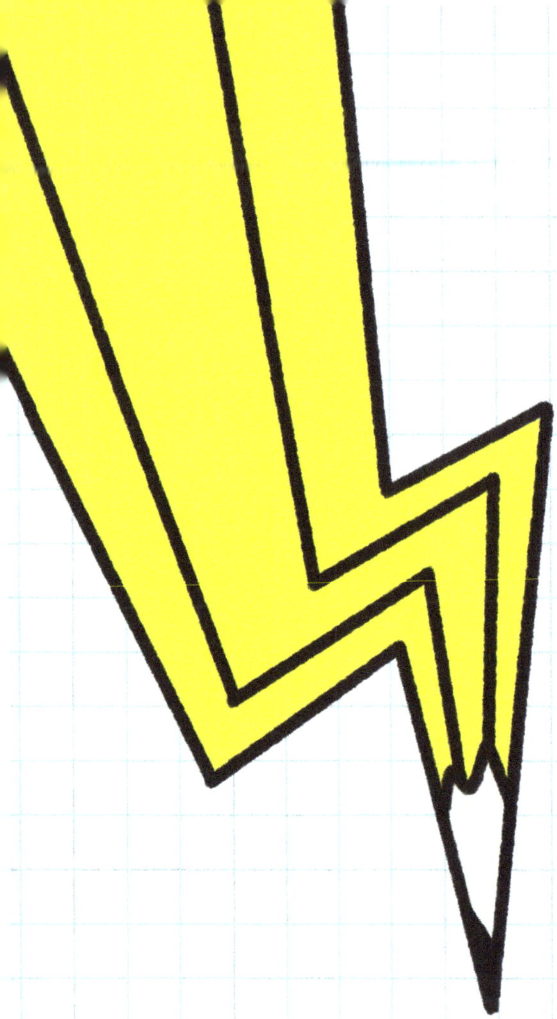

Ideas

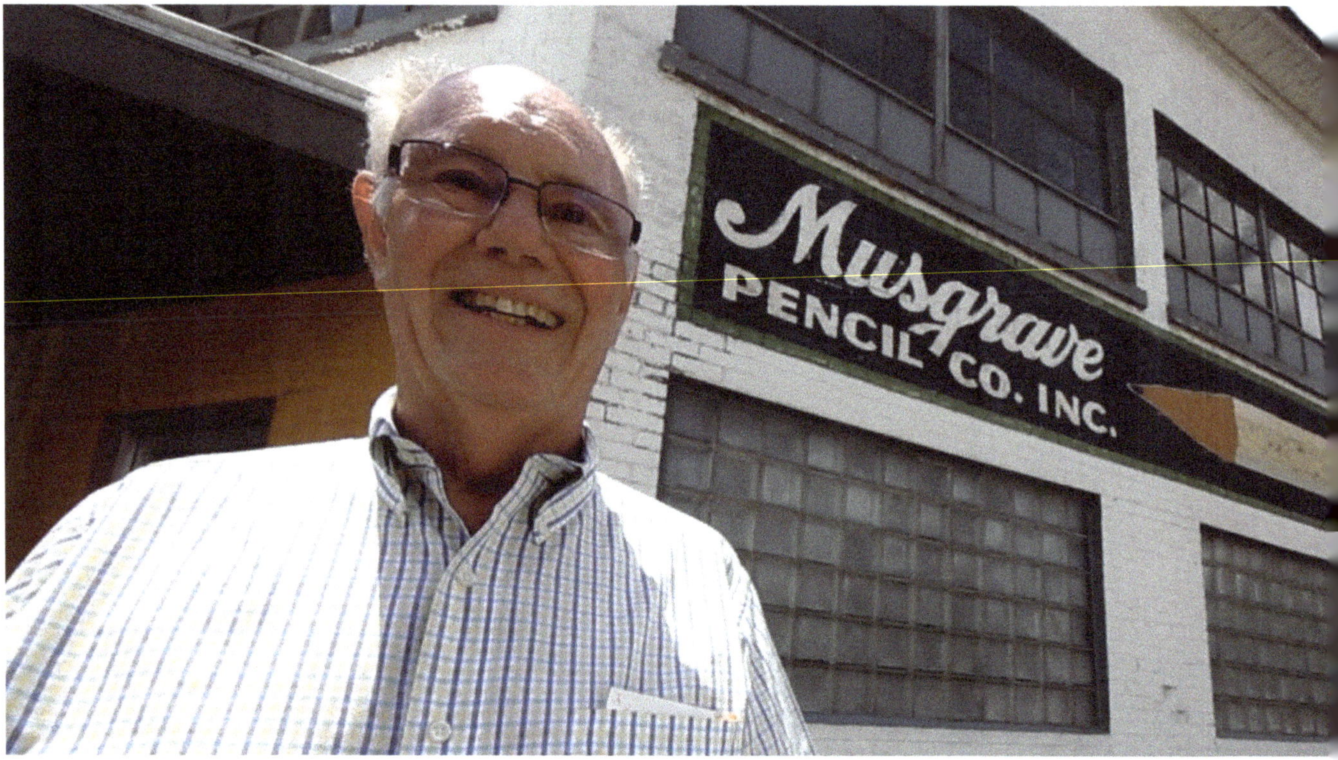

Manufacturing the Pencil

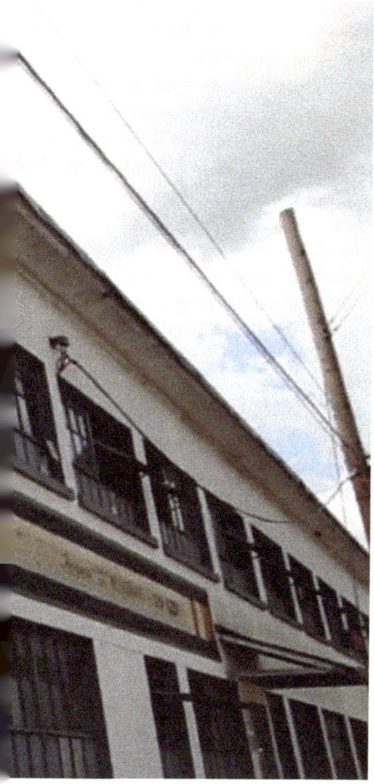

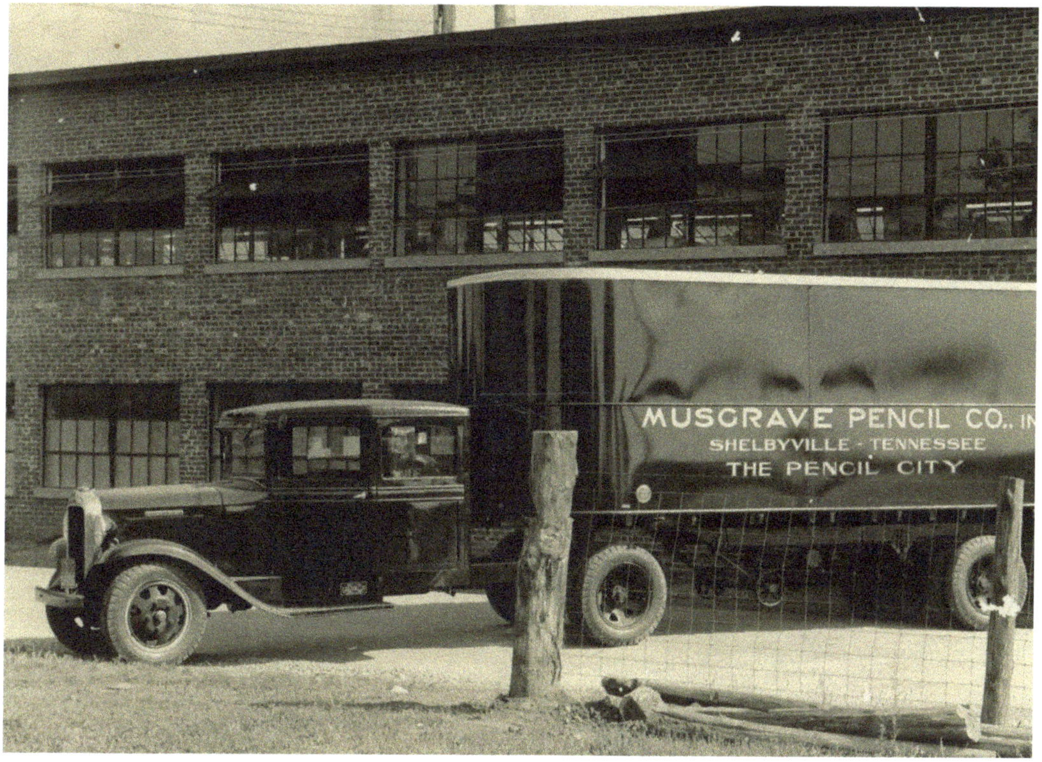

Henry Hulan, President of Musgrave Pencils, one of the last pencil manufacturers in the US

The pencil manufacturing process is fairly simple, but there are a lot of steps involved. If you counted all the steps to making a pencil, you'd probably have fifty or sixty different steps because you've got two pieces of wood that are glued together, that are grooved, and shaped, and painted. You've got ferrules, which is the metal tip on the pencil. You've got erasers. You've got paint. You've got different packaging products.

It's a fairly complicated process once you really get into it. We're working in thousandths of an inch because the pencils have to be either completely round or a hexagon pencil has to have the flat sides so it's printable, and we really have to watch that.

The manufacturing process is a pretty good process because you start with a slat that is grooved, and shaped, and clamped. Then it's shaped out into

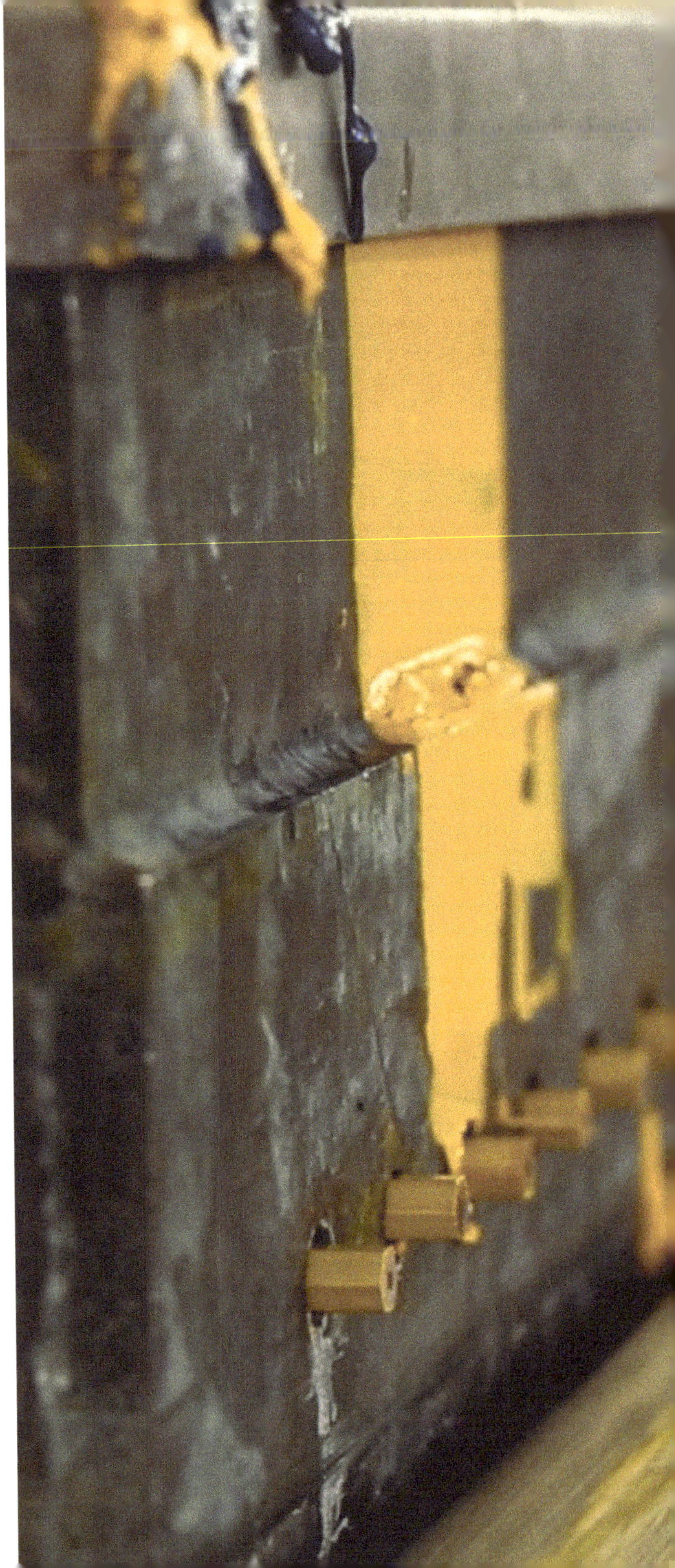

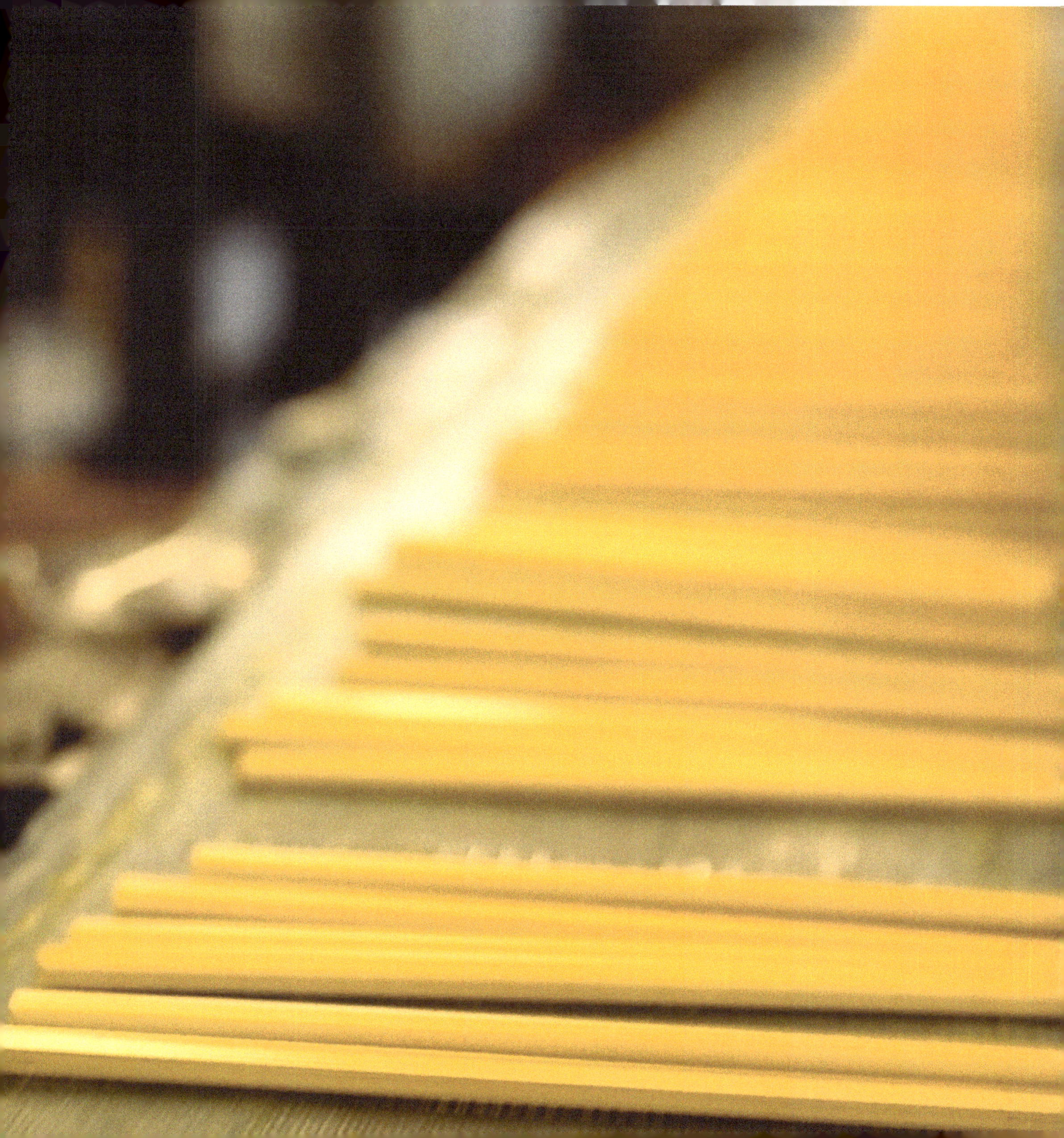

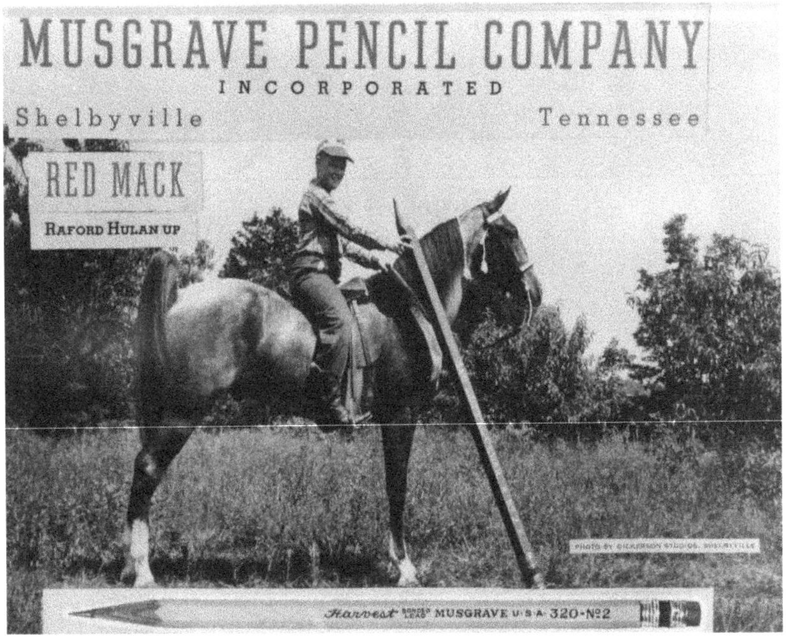
MUSGRAVE PENCIL COMPANY
INCORPORATED
Shelbyville
Tennessee
RED MACK
RAFORD HULAN UP
Harvest MUSGRAVE U·S·A· 320-№2

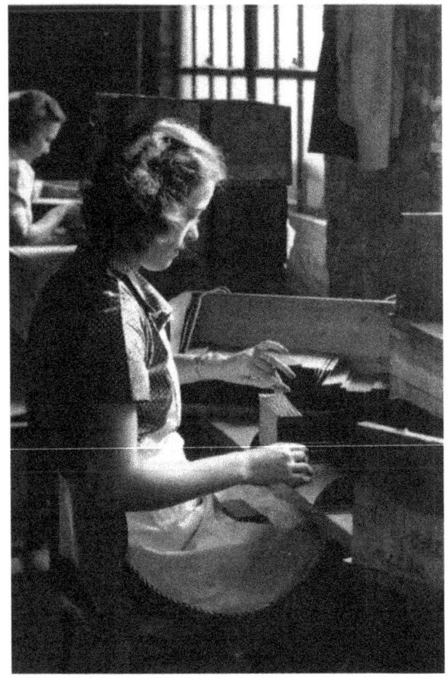

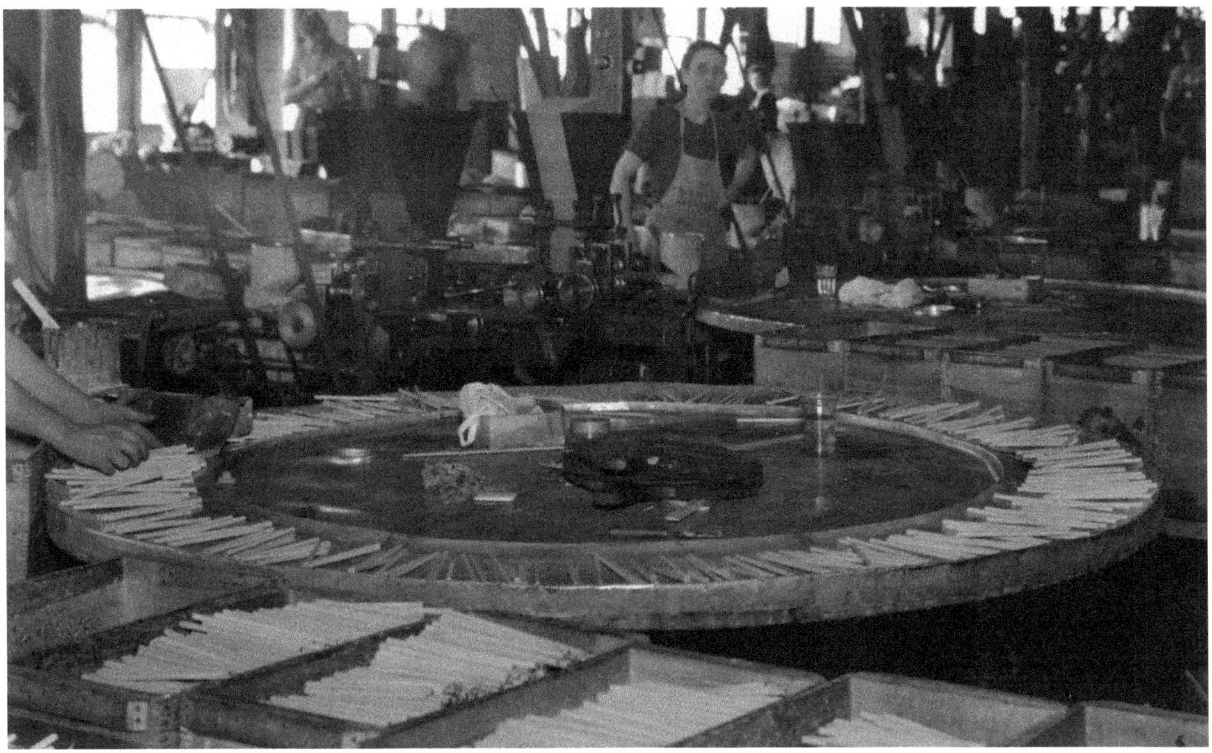

what we call a raw pencil. Then it goes to another department where it's painted, which is a really interesting process because pencils will have anywhere from five to nine coats of paint, whether it's paint or clear polish. To get the type of finish we want on it, it takes a lot of thin coats of paint. We're selling a printable surface, or using a printable surface, so it has to be smooth and shiny.

From there, you go to the printing process, and then you go into the tipping process, where you put the ferrule and the erasers on. Then the packaging process. A lot of different machines are used in the manufacturing process.

The industry itself settled in Middle-Tennessee because of the availability of Tennessee red cedar at the time. Then, once the pencil industry settled there, the core manufacturers, the eraser manufacturers, and the paint manufacturers eventually settled in Mid-Tennessee, too, so they would be close to their vendors.

Pencil manufacturing in the United States has sort of dwindled because the larger pencil manufacturers that have always controlled and been the big players in the market have been diversified enough to where they can have factories offshore, so they've left the United States, mostly because of cost. Musgrave Pencil Company felt like we could manufacture a product in the United States and still be competitive with enough of our different items to stay here, and we think that's important.

Challenges

Looking back at the manufacturing processes again, it's the little things that are always a headache, like in any industry. People change materials, change paints, change this and that. Probably the biggest problem that I can go back and really put a finger on would be the bonding of the wood and the graphite core.

In the manufacturing process, a pencil's core starts out with two wood slats. The slats are grooved, and then glue is put in the grooves and the graphite core is aligned within those grooves. Then another slat that has grooves put together in what we call a sandwich. Then it's clamped and stays overnight before it's shaped the next day into individual pencils. Sometimes either the glue or the gluing process that we use doesn't work, and glue will not get on both sides and around the core. When you sharpen the pencil, the core will break off or fall out, or the wood will come apart. The thing about it is it might happen on two pencils out of every nine. It's a real headache. That part is one thing you have to watch closely.

Holding On

If you look at a pencil that we made in 1923 and look at a pencil coming off the paint line today, it's going to look the same. It's the processes that have changed a little bit. They've gotten more mechanized. There isn't quite as much handiwork now than there used to be. The pencil has changed, but of course the hexagon and round shape has not. People use round jumbo pencils in the lower grades still. Our carpenter pencils are

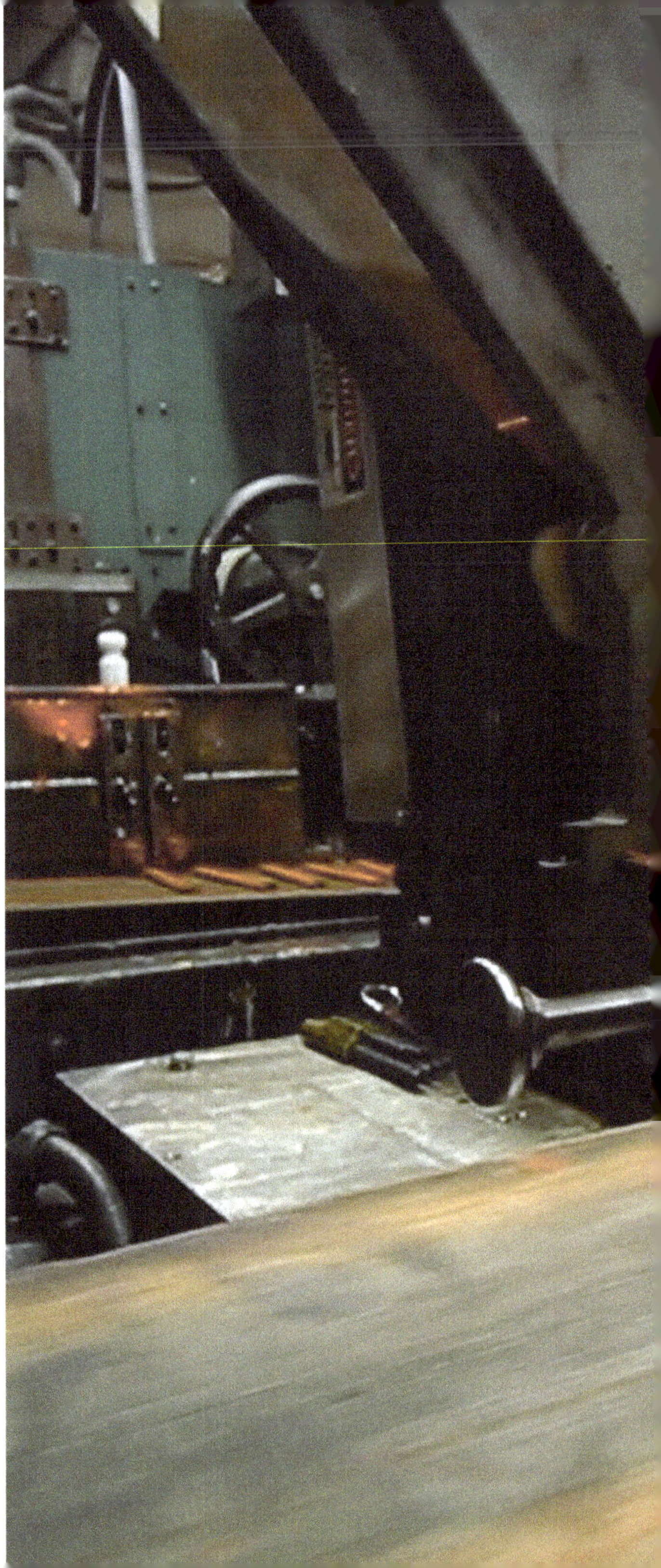

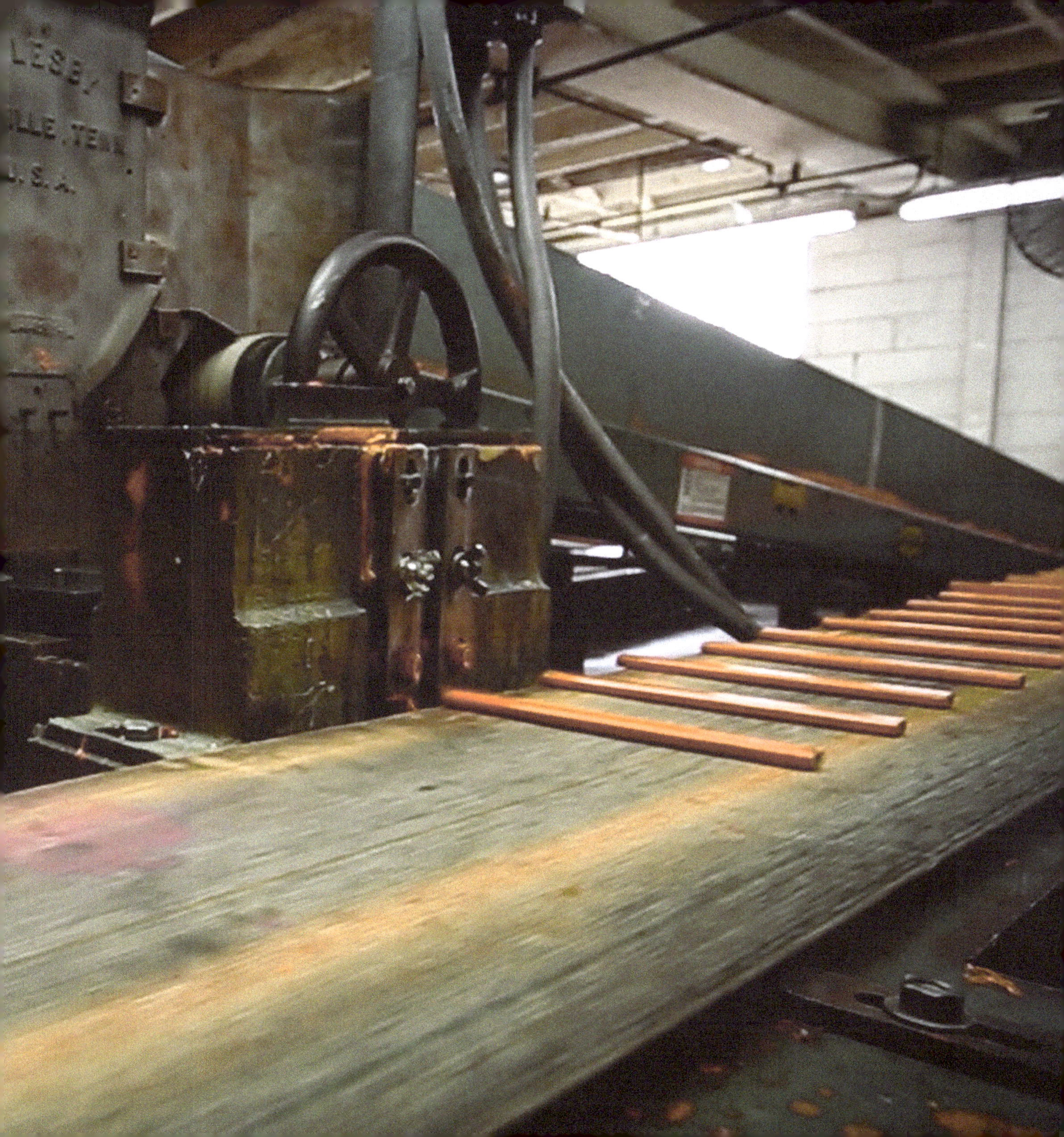

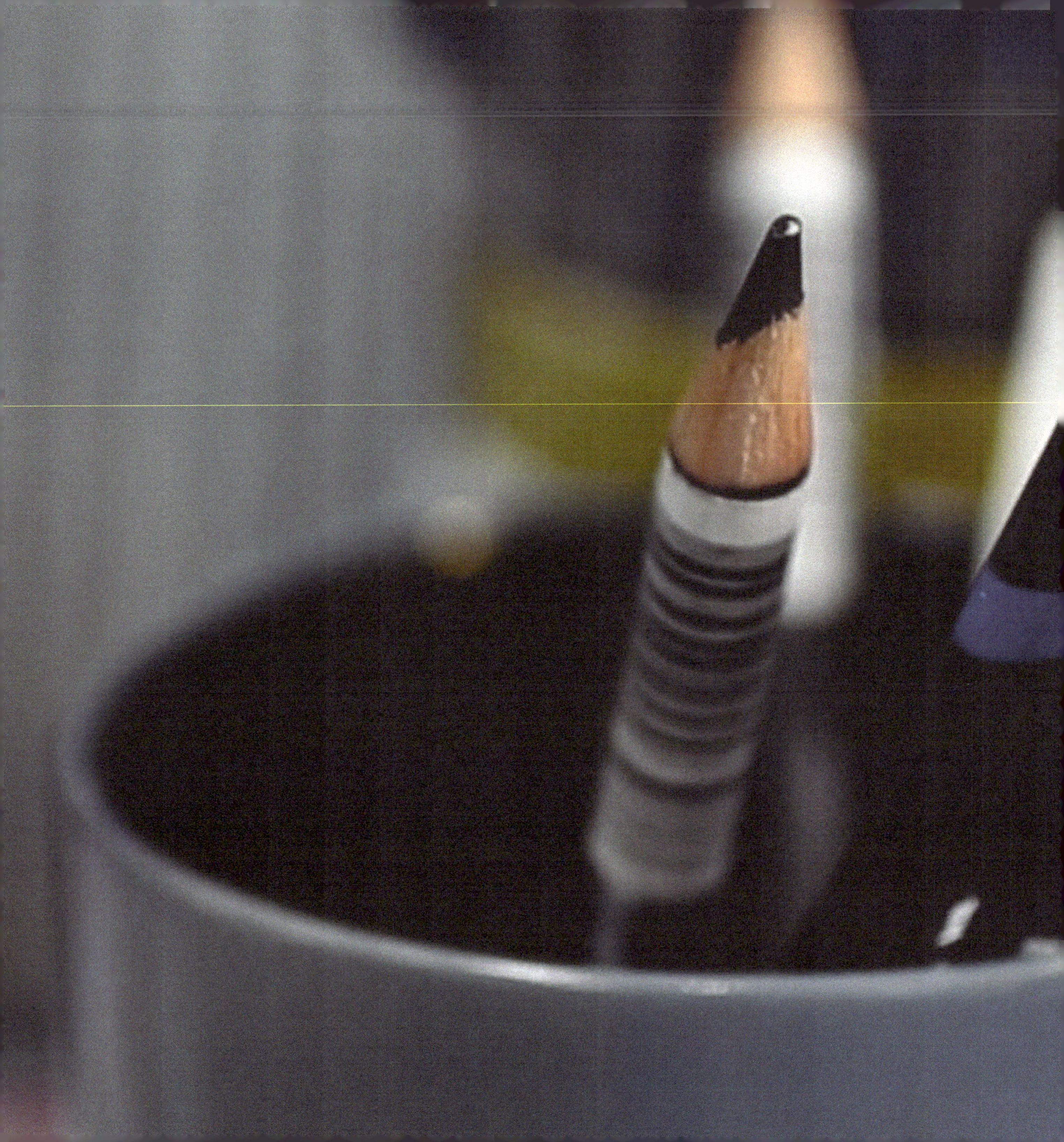

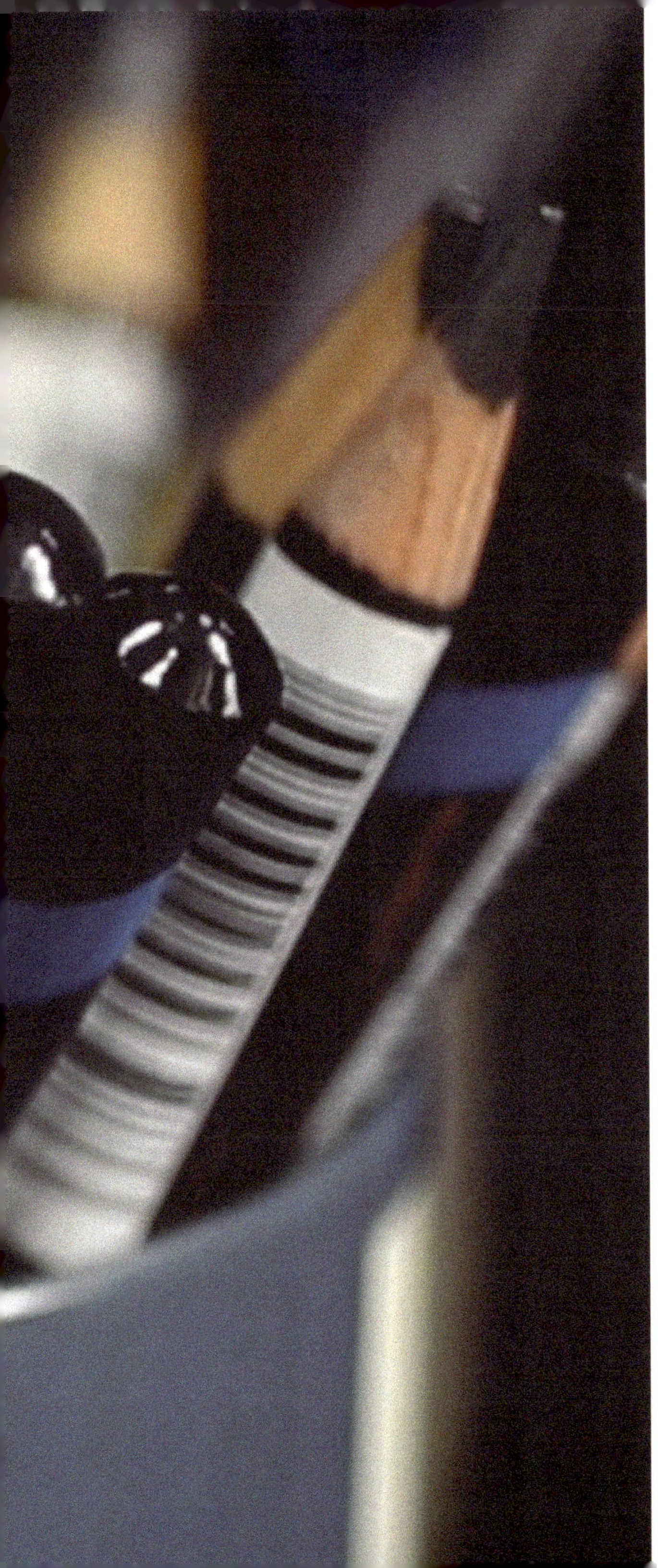

popular, but they're still basically made the same way. The processes, like I said, have changed a little bit, but it's an interesting operation to see. Where the speed has changed some, the process has not.

No. 2

A No. 2 pencil is the most popular core degree. A core is a mixture of graphite, clay, and water. A lot of people call it a lead pencil, though there is no lead in the pencil. Never has been, just a graphite core. No. 2 is a medium degree, and it easily makes a good, solid mark on a piece of paper. Easily erasable. The other degrees people use in a lot of different drawings are anything from a No. 1, which is softer than a No. 2, while 3 and 4 are harder. There are eighteen degrees of drawing pencils, and they go from very, very soft to very, very hard. That's for sketching and different types of mechanical drawings—things like that.

Pencils play an important part of the past, the present, and the future of the world, as far as I'm concerned. It's a simple tool, yet it's just so diverse.

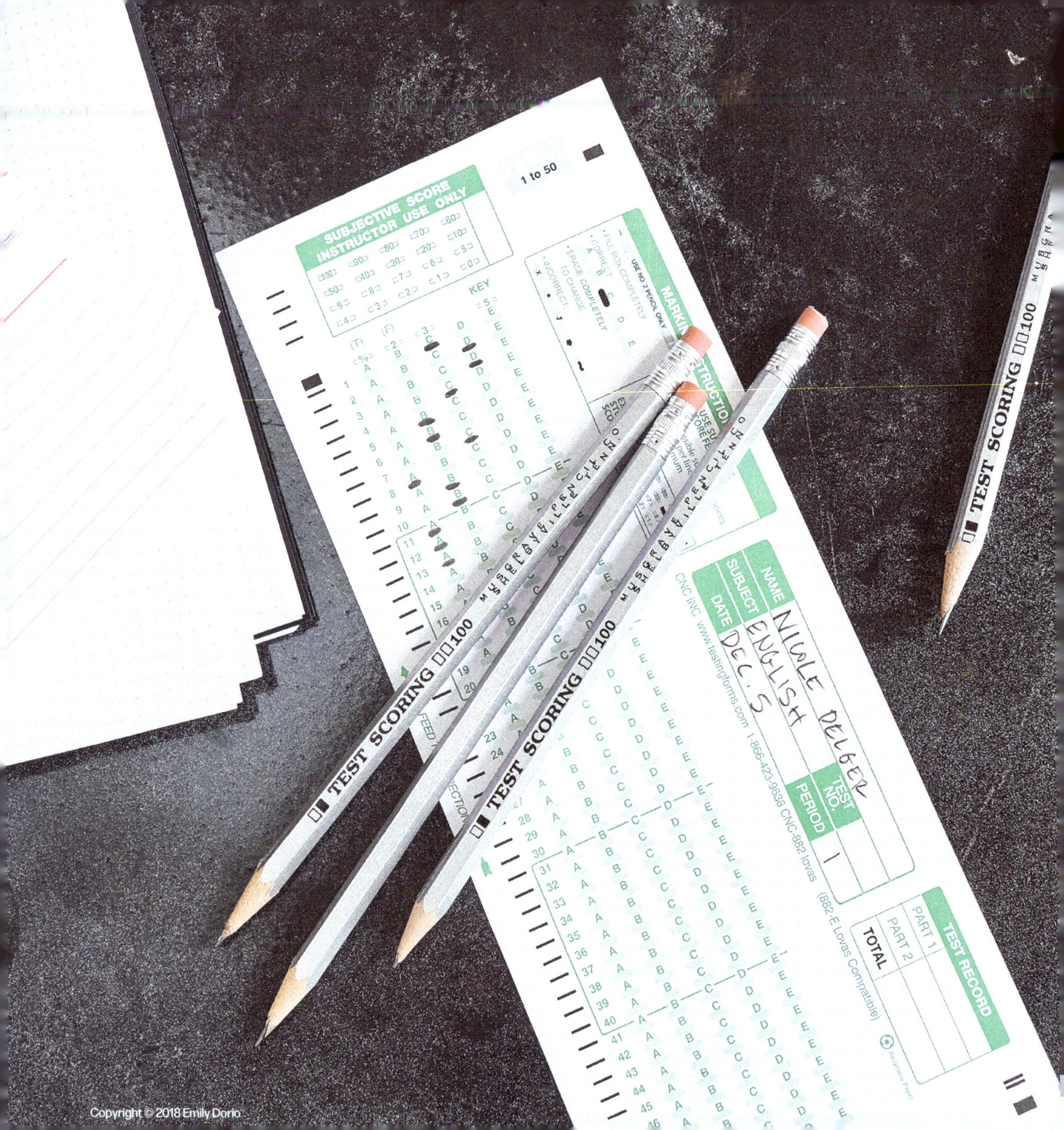

SUBJECTIVE SCORE
INSTRUCTOR USE ONLY
1 to 50
KEY
NAME
SUBJECT
DATE
ENGLISH
DEC. 5
TEST NO.
PERIOD
CNC INC www.testingforms.com 1-866-423-9638 CNC-882 lovas
(882-E Lovas Compatible)
TEST RECORD
PART 1
PART 2
TOTAL
TEST SCORING 100

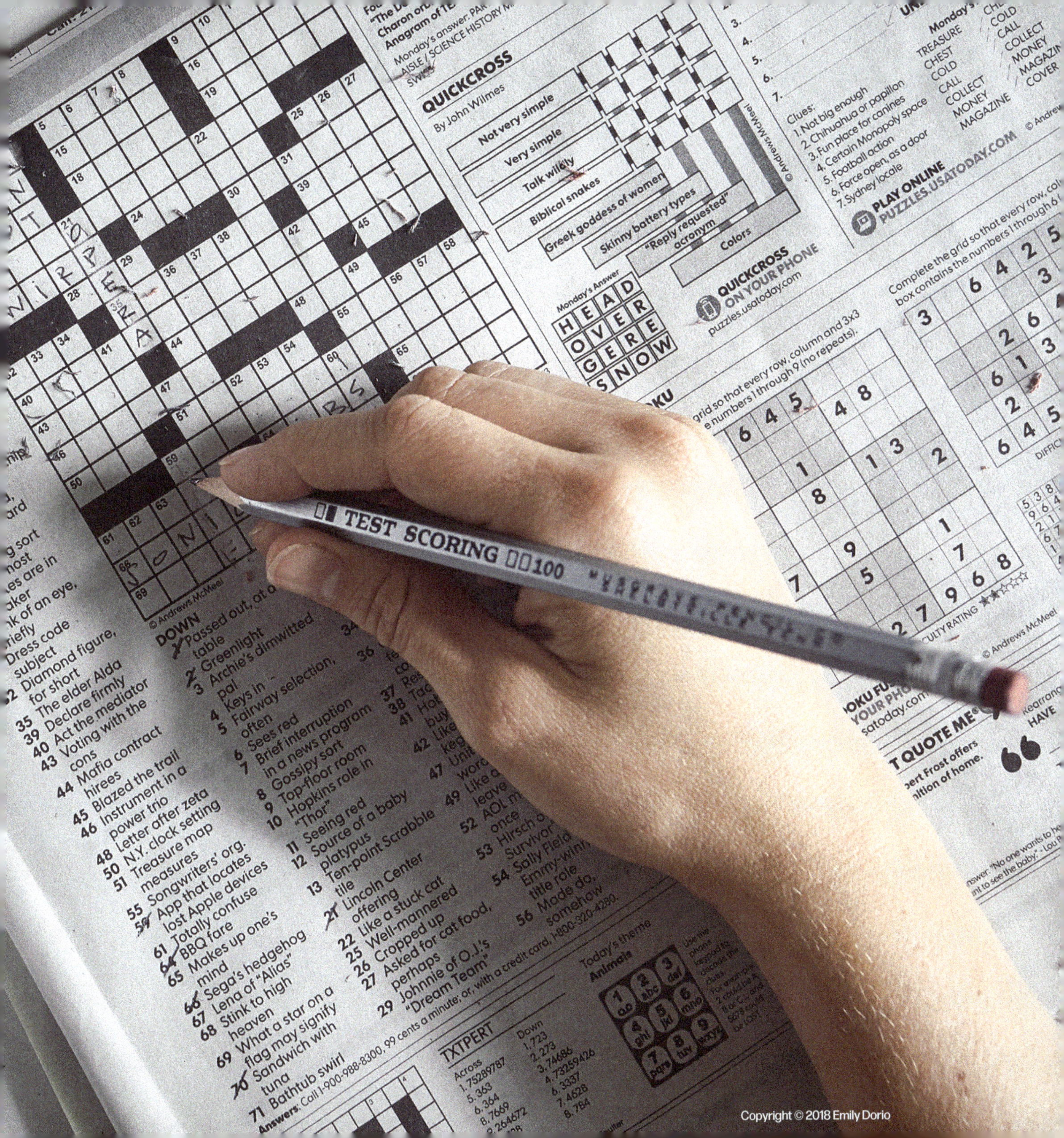
QUICKCROSS
By John Wilmes
Not very simple
Very simple
Talk wildly
Biblical snakes
Greek goddess of women
Skinny battery types
"Reply requested" acronym
Colors
Monday's Answer
HEAD
OVER
GERE
SNOW
QUICKCROSS ON YOUR PHONE
puzzles.usatoday.com
PLAY ONLINE
PUZZLES.USATODAY.COM
Clues:
1. Not big enough
2. Chihuahua or papillon
3. Fun place for canines
4. Certain Monopoly space
5. Football action
6. Force open, as a door
7. Sydney locale
Monday's
TREASURE
CHEST
COLD
CALL
COLLECT
MONEY
MAGAZINE
TEST SCORING 100
DOWN
1 Passed out, at a table
2 Greenlight
3 Archie's dimwitted pal
4 Keys in
5 Fairway selection, often
6 Sees red
7 Brief interruption in a news program
8 Gossipy sort
9 Top-floor room
10 Hopkins role in "Thor"
11 Seeing red
12 Source of a baby platypus
13 Ten-point Scrabble tile
21 Lincoln Center offering
22 Like a stuck cat
25 Well-mannered
26 Cropped up
27 Asked for cat food, perhaps
29 Johnnie of O.J.'s "Dream Team"
Today's theme
Animals
TXTPERT
Across
Down

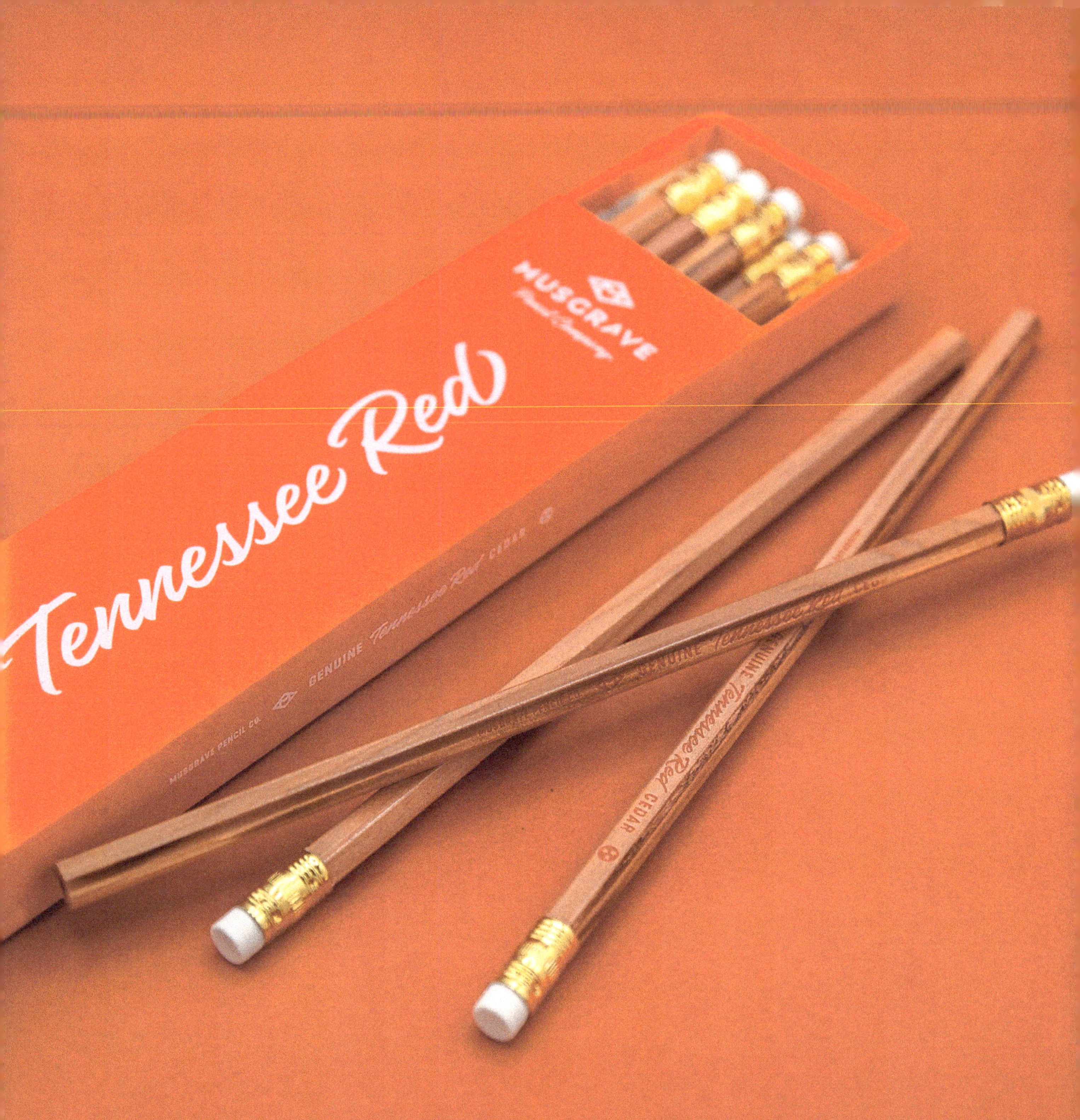
MUSGRAVE
Pencil Company
Tennessee Red
MUSGRAVE PENCIL CO.
GENUINE Tennessee Red CEDAR
GENUINE Tennessee Red CEDAR

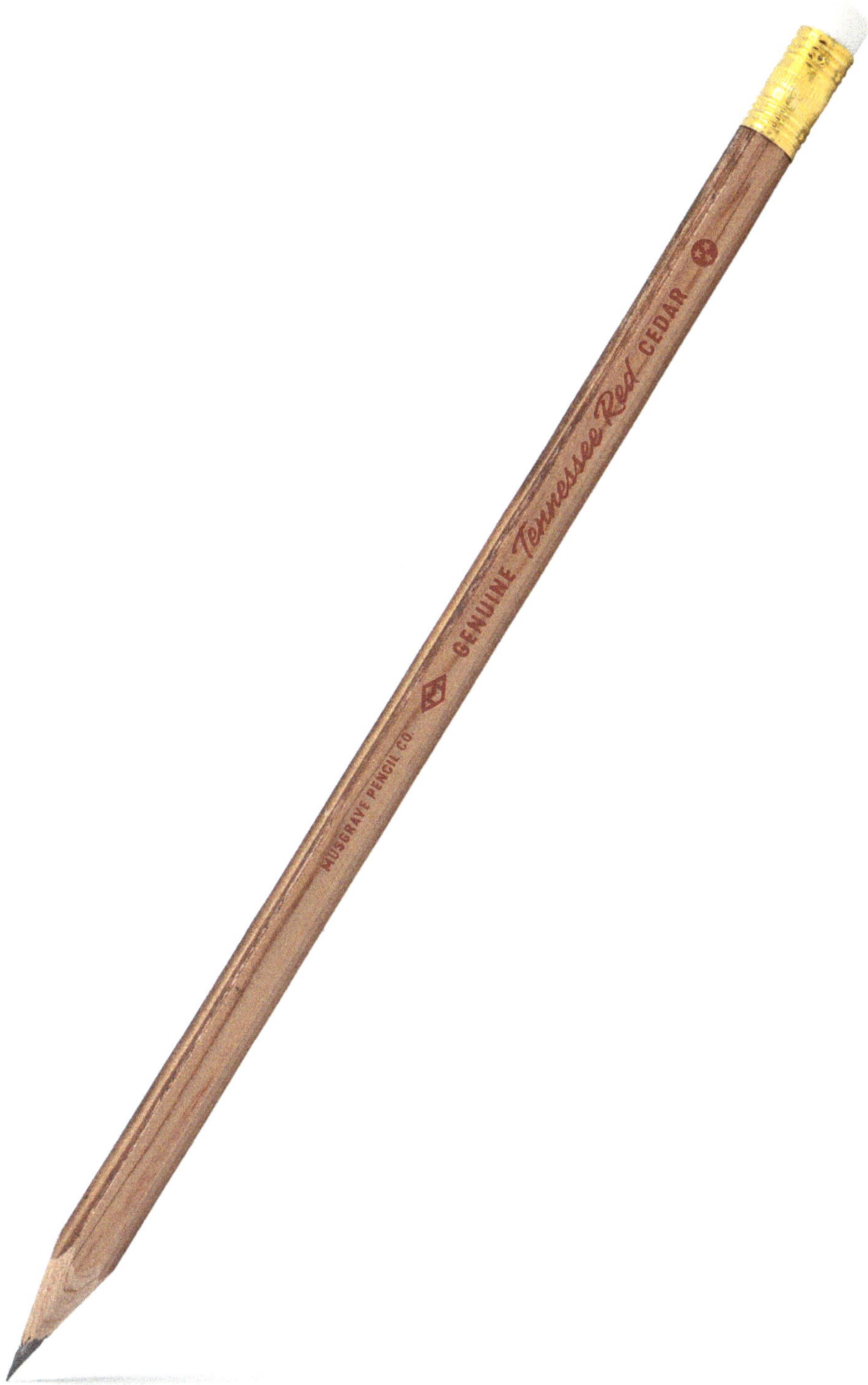
MUSGRAVE PENCIL CO
GENUINE Tennessee Red CEDAR

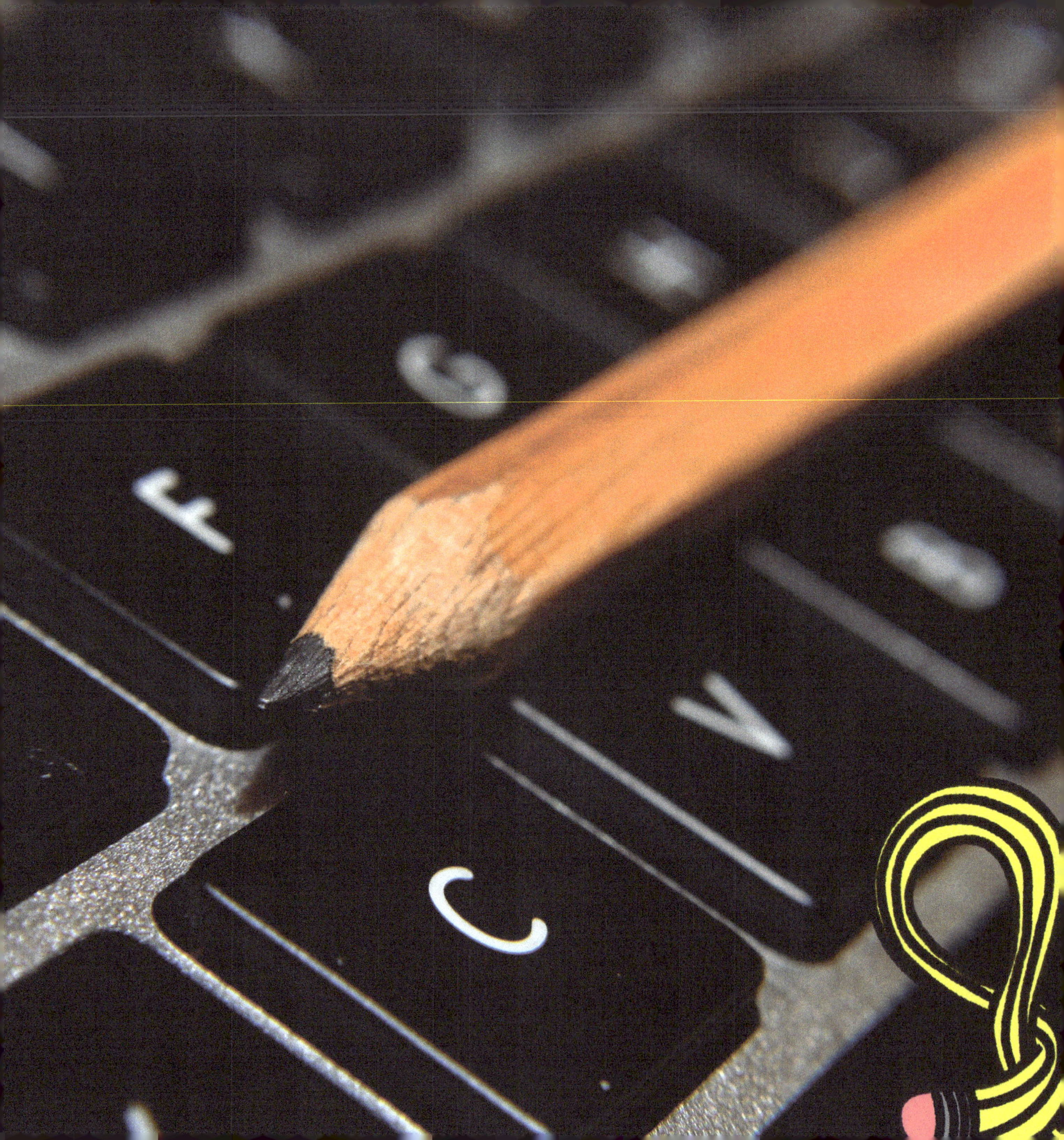

Distortion

deliberate alteration of forms to create unique and expressive effects

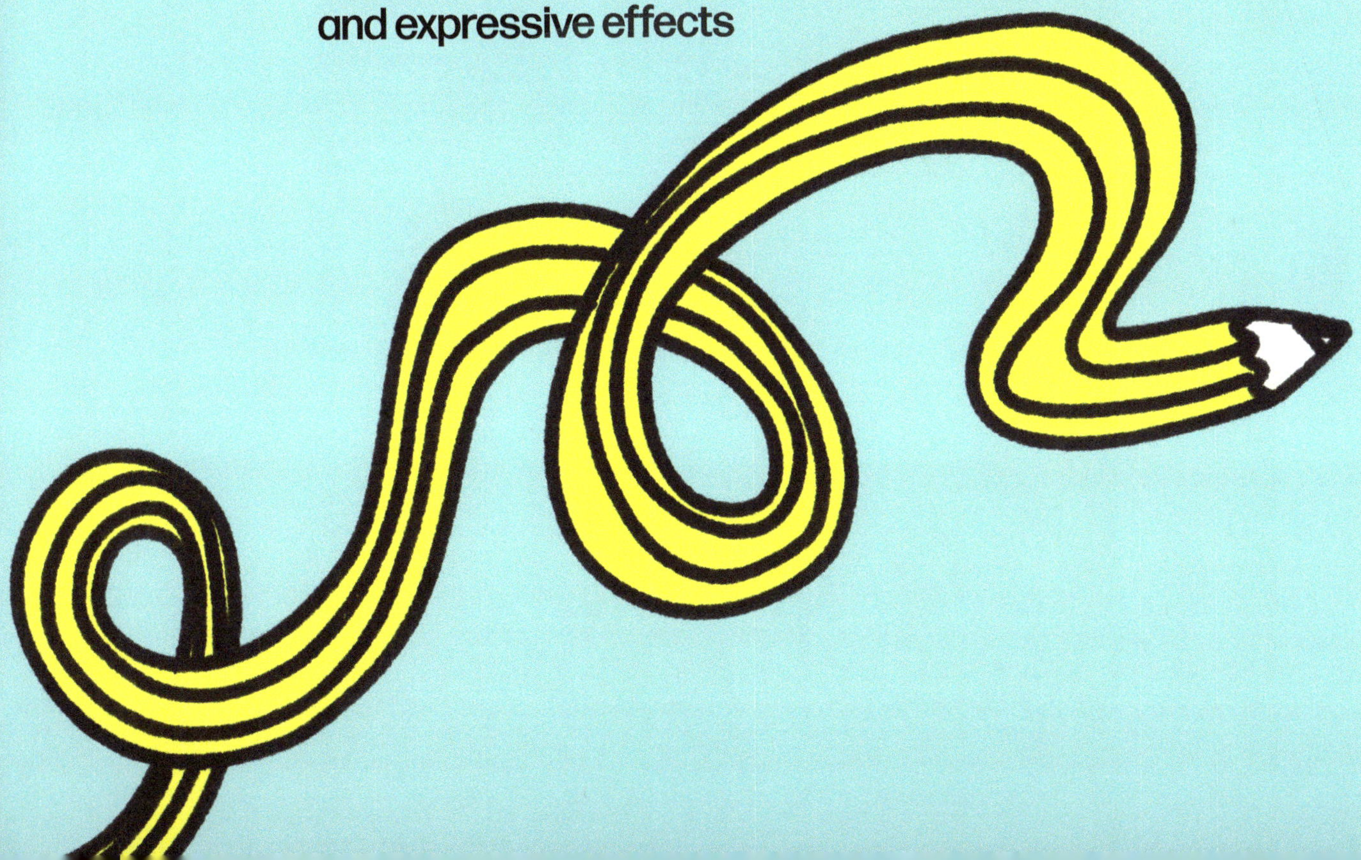

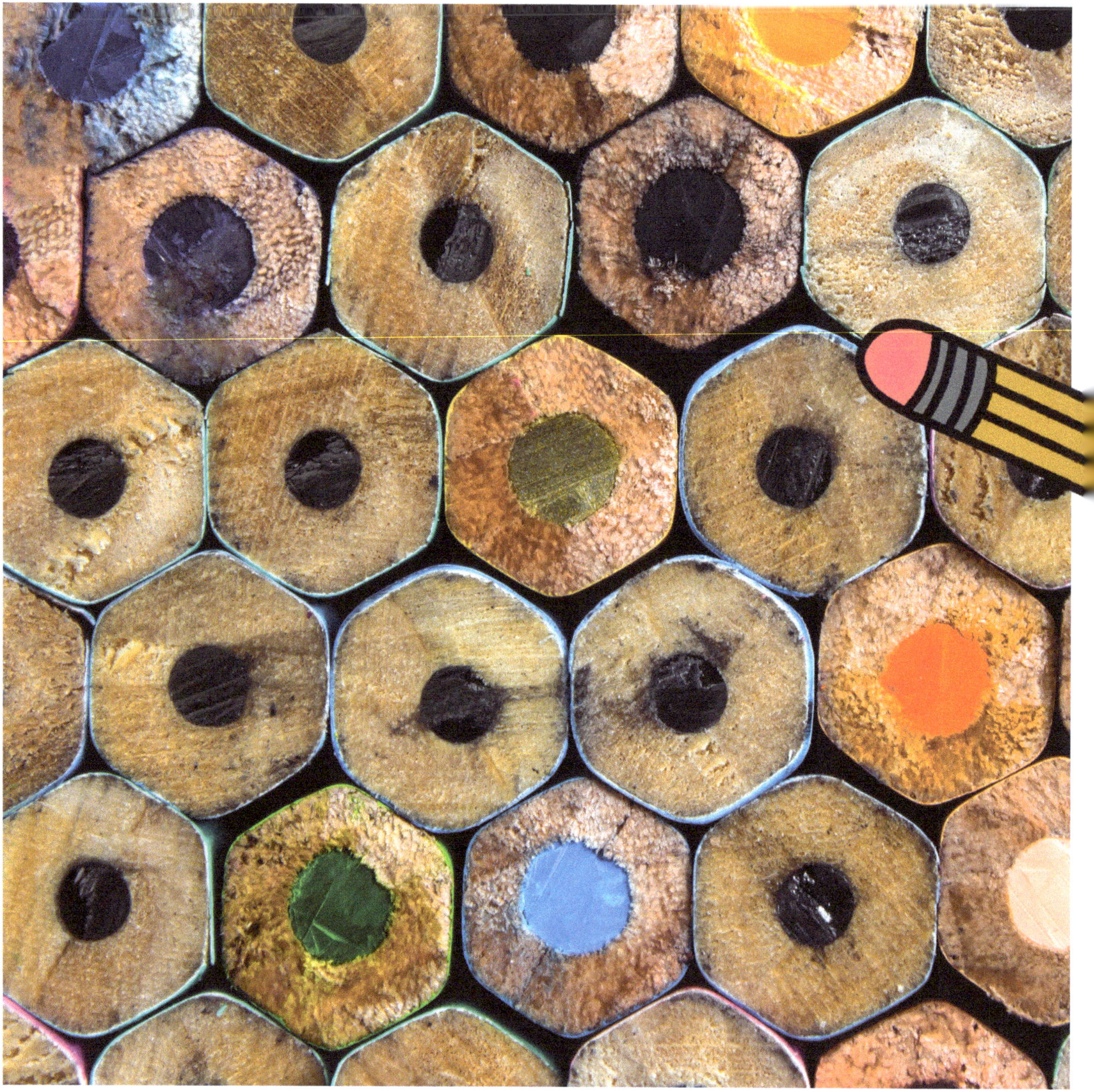

A Blast from the Past

Dr. Art Hunt, Media Ecologist

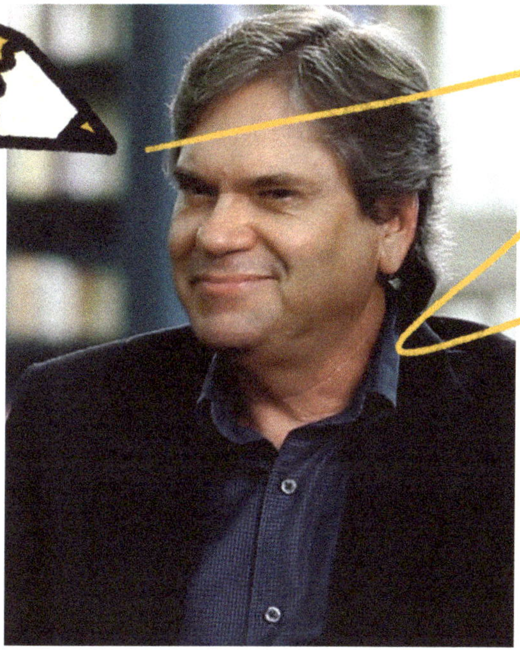

"For me, the beauty of the pencil is the eraser, which sets it apart from a pen. With an eraser, you can erase your mistakes, and they're gone. Unlike a pen, you can only mark out that word - the eraser is forgiving. It's grace."

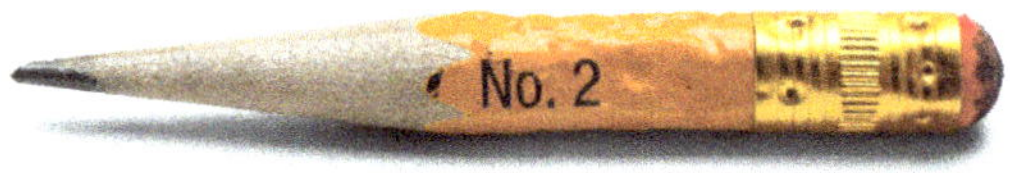

Thinking back on my own first-grade experience, I have vivid memories of taking that big pencil—it was a big, fat pencil (with our small hands, we could not properly grasp a small, skinny No. 2 pencil)—forming my letters and looking at the letters up on the wall, making my letters look exactly like that. Those are my earliest memories of learning my alphabet and how important it was to actually write my letters by hand.

My understanding now is that people are doing away with writing by hand, especially cursive writing, which concerns me a great deal. For hundreds of years, the ability to write, the process of writing, was a part of a person's education. Now that the computer has come in, it has short-circuited this writing process. And I'm not so sure this is for the better.

There are some people who have chosen not to compose with a computer. Wendell Berry, the well-known essayist, farmer, philosopher, and agrarian, decided he would not use a computer. In fact, he wrote an essay called "Why I Will Not Use a Computer." Now Berry writes in a treehouse. He takes a pencil and a pad and goes up there to write.

In his book, *What Are People For*, he talks about how, in a technological society like ours, there is a disconnect between the body and what we do in everyday life. He says:

"In speaking of language, we have it palpably in our mouths. It is in our language, our tongue, writing it—we shape it with our hands. Reading aloud what we have written, as we must do if we are writing carefully, our language passes in at the eyes, out at the mouth, in at the ears. The words are immersed and steeped in the senses of the body before they make sense to the mind. They cannot make sense to the mind until they have made sense to the body."

He believes there's a new Gnosticism that thinks of the body as being inferior, in comparison to mechanical standards. But he doesn't compose using a computer. This is deliberate because he wants to make full use of his body. He says that language, when you think about it in the writing process, is in our mouths. Then we shape it with our hands. Then, if we're a good writer and if we're careful, we'll read it back to ourselves. And so again, we are hearing it out loud. It's going back into our ears, so it's not just a mental process; it's a bodily process.

In a technological society—in a machine society—there's a tendency to want to downplay our bodies and think of machines, or machine standards, as being better or superior than the old processes of using our hands, and even our minds to some extent. There's no question that the rise of the pencil, and also the rise of literacy rates in the American colonies, happened at the same time. Literacy rates were as high as 95% in the colonies for males and almost 65% with females.

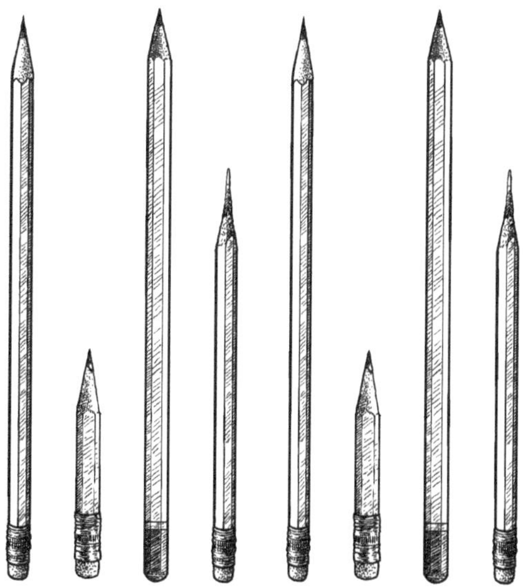

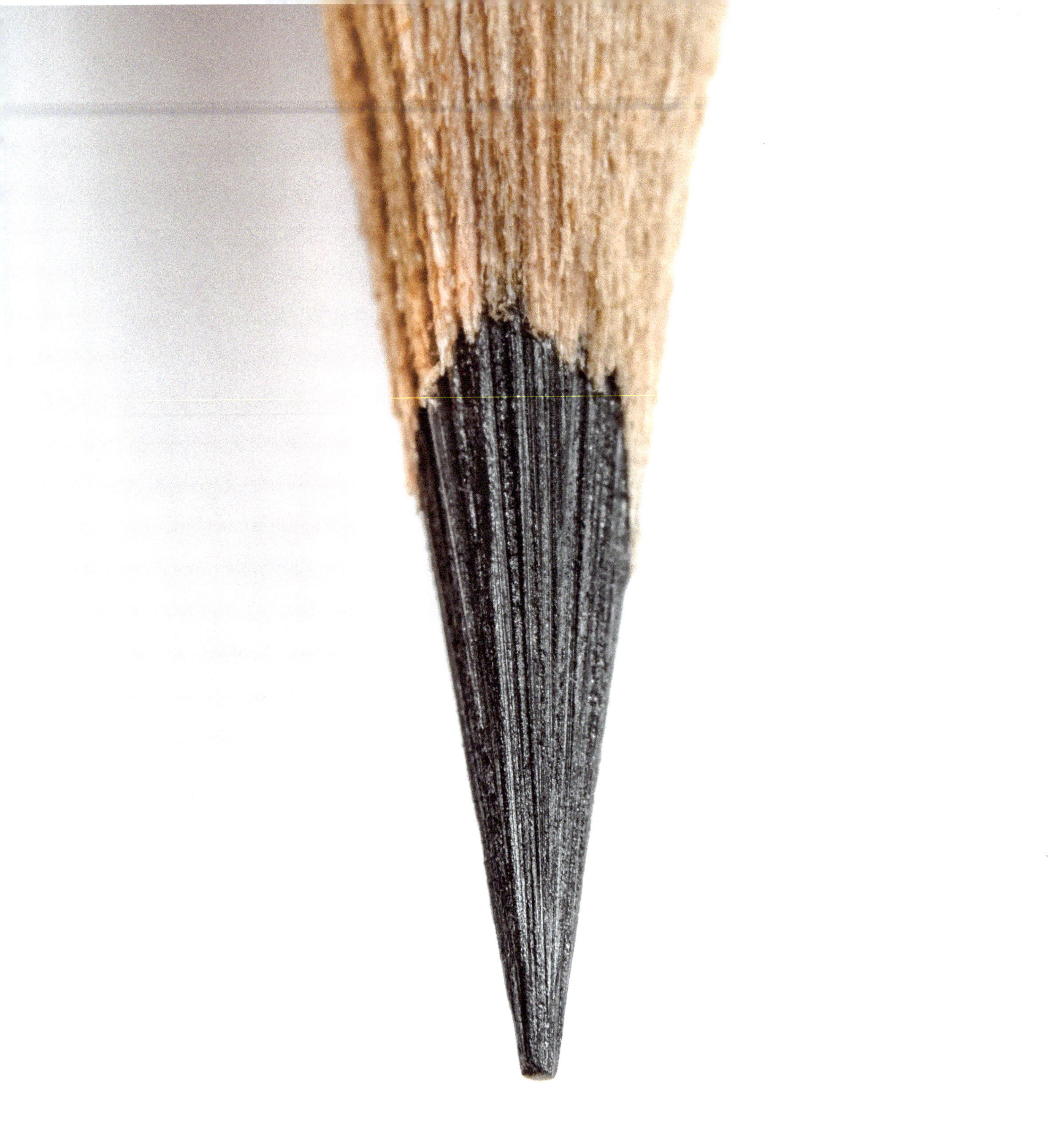

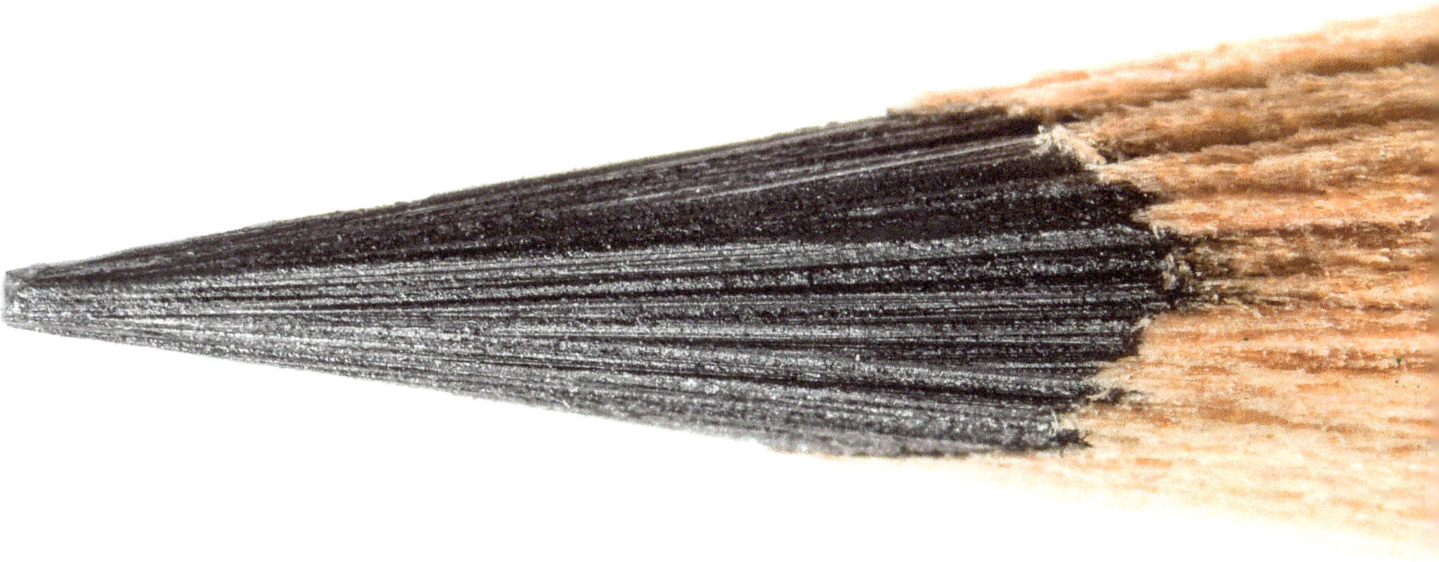

I can't imagine a child learning how to read and write without a pencil, but I suppose it could happen, where we would go right from learning how to speak, into school, and then composing on a keyboard, skipping writing altogether—skip the pencil altogether. I think a lot would be lost if we did that. Yet, the pencil is fast becoming in the way of the dinosaur, so we may not be that far from it.

My understanding of literacy is that there's a connection between writing, the body, and being able to read, as well. Of course, I equate the pencil with the ability to write, the ability to write with literacy, and literacy with education. You throw the pencil out, and you're changing traditional education.

When society talks about being an educated person, that's a person who can both read and write well. I'm not so sure that our schools are emphasizing reading as much as we should be. I also can't help to think that it's because there are so many other things vying for their attention, like new media.

I think the pencil is a metaphor for literacy, though I'm not so sure the keyboard is. The mouse isn't the best metaphor for literacy, either. A mouse, you click, but a pencil allows us to form words on a page.

The pencil is slowly being replaced with the keyboard in our schools, which is not a good thing. The ability to be able to put your words down on paper, to write in print, and to write in cursive facilitates thinking and the entire writing process. The mouse and the keyboard will short-circuit that.

In the future, we might see some people who are deliberate in trying to retain some of those old technologies. I can see there might be people who will want to revert back to the pencil. There might be people who will want to revert back to letter writing. There are some people who just absolutely refuse to use certain technologies. I don't have a GPS system. Why? I like getting lost. There's a mystery to it.

You are Being Childish

The pencil might be on the short end of the stick when it comes to technological advancement. I feel like the pencil is probably going to be replaced with the keyboard and the mouse. And as we are seeing the end of childhood, we are also seeing the end of the pencil. Hence, when it comes to the loss of the pencil, we might compare it to the loss of childhood.

Neil Postman wrote a book titled The Disappearance of Childhood, in which he made the claim that our modern notions of childhood came because we decided to educate children, to set them aside so they could read and write. But now children are exposed to the adult world via media. And so, the end of the pencil is a little bit like the end of childhood.

Down the road, people are going to realize they are losing out because of some of our new technologies. There will be people who actually rebel. We're already seeing this to some degree. Homeschooling is a type of rebelling.

There are people who are going to want to preserve the traditional modes of education. Whether it be in a homeschool, a private school, or a religious school, they're going to take their pencils, and they're going to keep them to preserve those old modes of learning—reading, writing, and arithmetic.

The worst-case scenario is that we will redefine education and literacy. That doesn't mean that, to be literate, you have to be able to read and write, that you'll have to be able to click. But that is not literacy in the way we have thought about it. Literacy has always been about being able to read and write. If that goes out the window, then our understanding of education goes out the window, too, at least of how we have perceived it for years. There is pressure to leave the old definition of literacy. It's out there.

Vanished

Writing is permanent, and writing is portable. However, digital communication is fleeting. It can easily disappear. It can easily be manipulated. It can be forgotten. We're spending quite a bit of time putting our libraries online by digitizing them, which is a concern. This concern has to do with being about to actually take a book off the shelf, or take your hand and put your thoughts on paper. There's a permanency to that. It's physical. It's more tangible. In the digital world, however, that disappears. It goes into the air. We used to teach our children how to write. That is to say, how to form letters on a page, to print. Then we would move them to cursive writing, which was the form that we would use to communicate our thoughts, to write letters, and to extend ourselves, extend our thoughts. But now we're composing on the screen more. There is a loss to that.

The call of the age is to do it quickly and get it out there. But writing slows things down. It allows you to meditate. It allows you to chew on the pencil. It allows you to take that eraser and reformulate the thought. It takes time to write. And that's not a bad thing. Reflection is not a bad thing. I'm afraid that the pressure is to just tap it out and get it out there, which is a loss for us.

There is a connection between writing and the body. The writing process is really a bodily experience. Taking a pencil and forming your letters is a better use of the body than tapping it out.

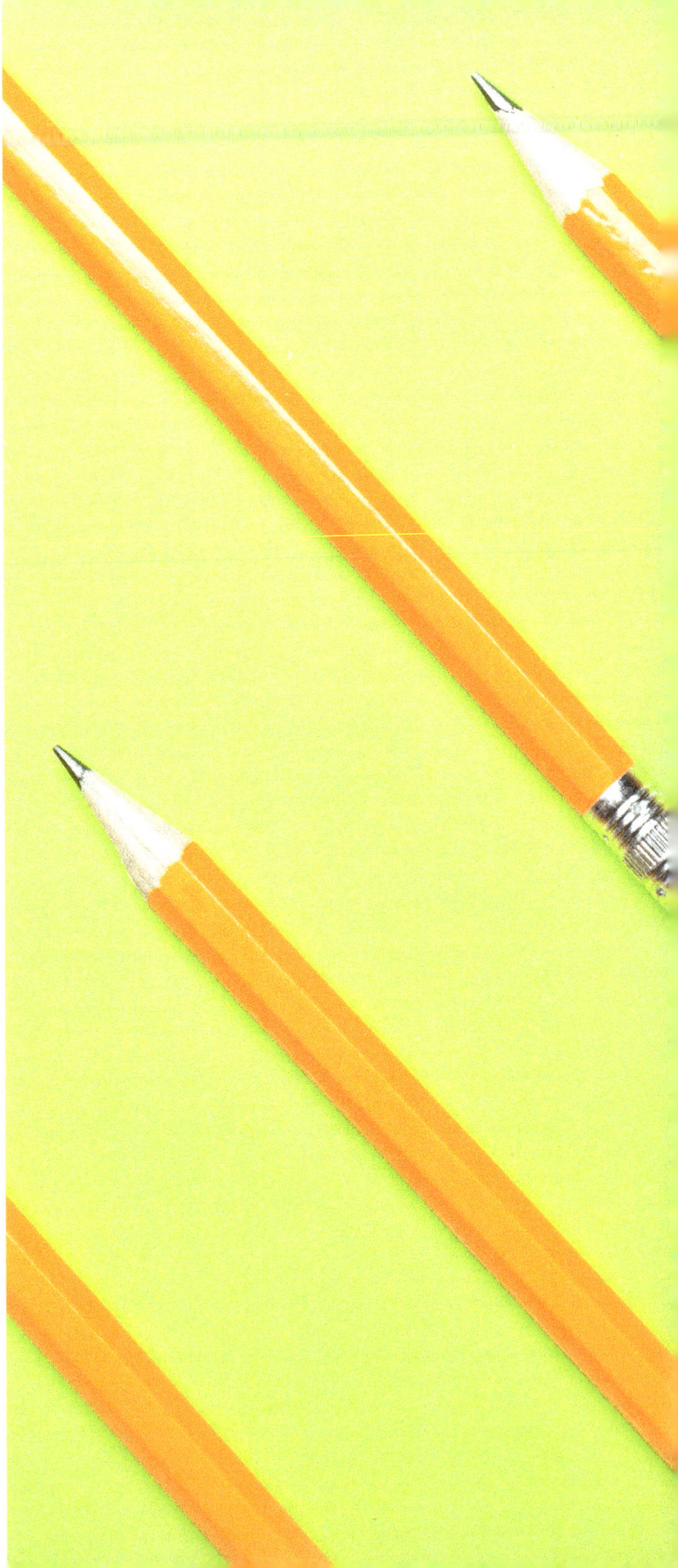

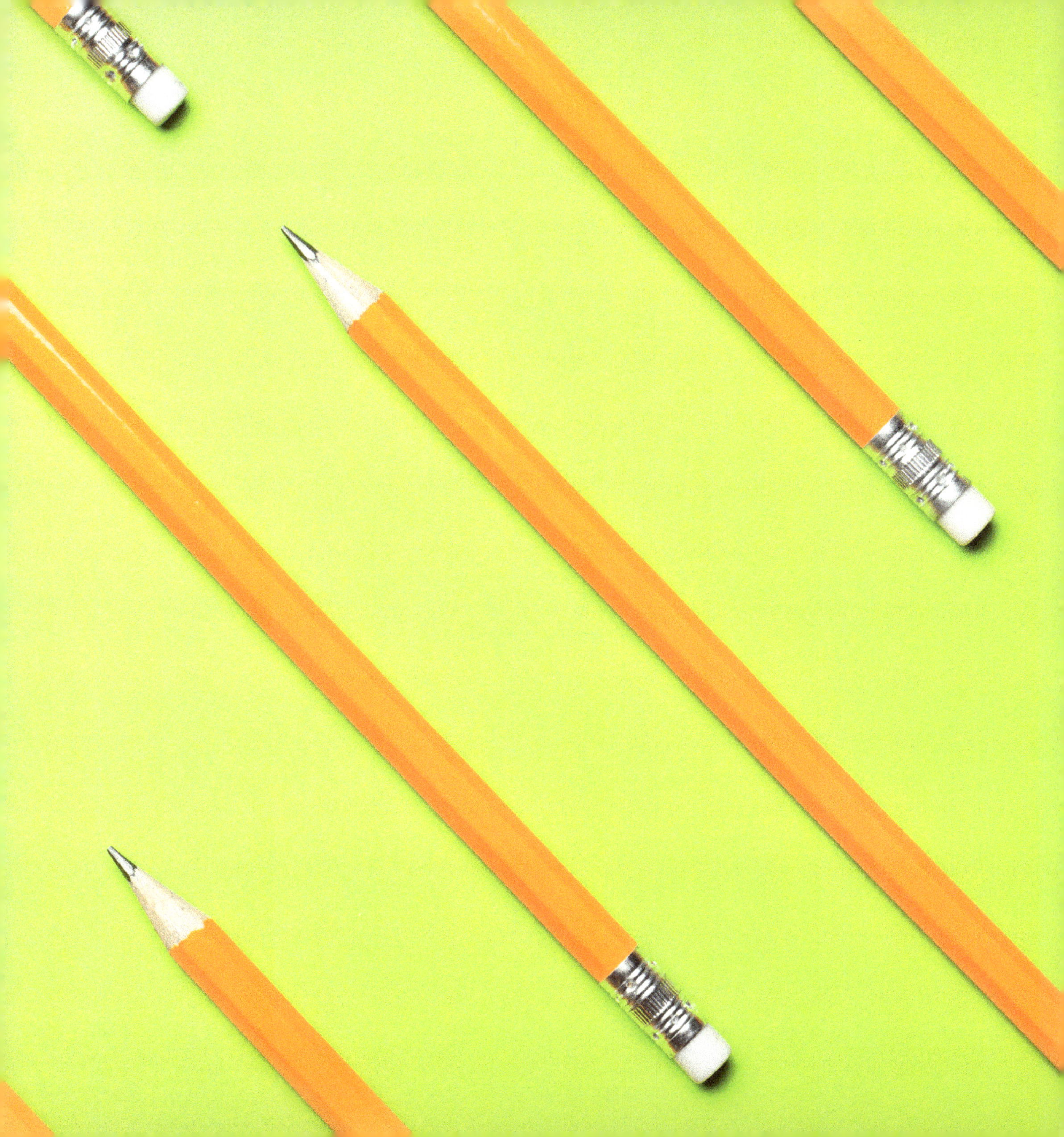

Aa Bb C

Ff Gg Hh

Ll Mm

Qq Rr S

Vv Ww X

1 2 3 4 5

! # $ %

c Dd Ee

Ii Jj Kk

n Oo Pp

s Tt Uu

x Yy Zz

7 8 9 0

'()*,-./

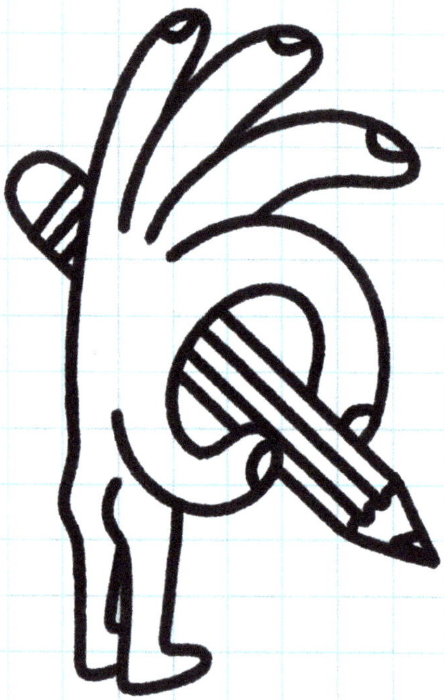

Ideas

You Say You Want a Revolution

Caroline Weaver,
CW Pencil Enterprise
(the only pencil shop in the world)

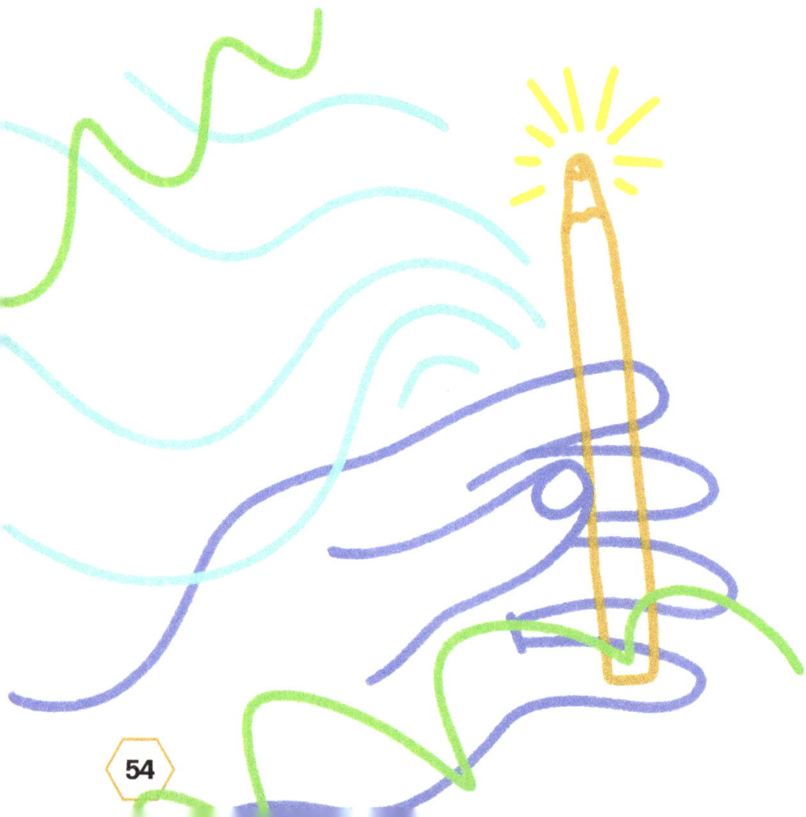

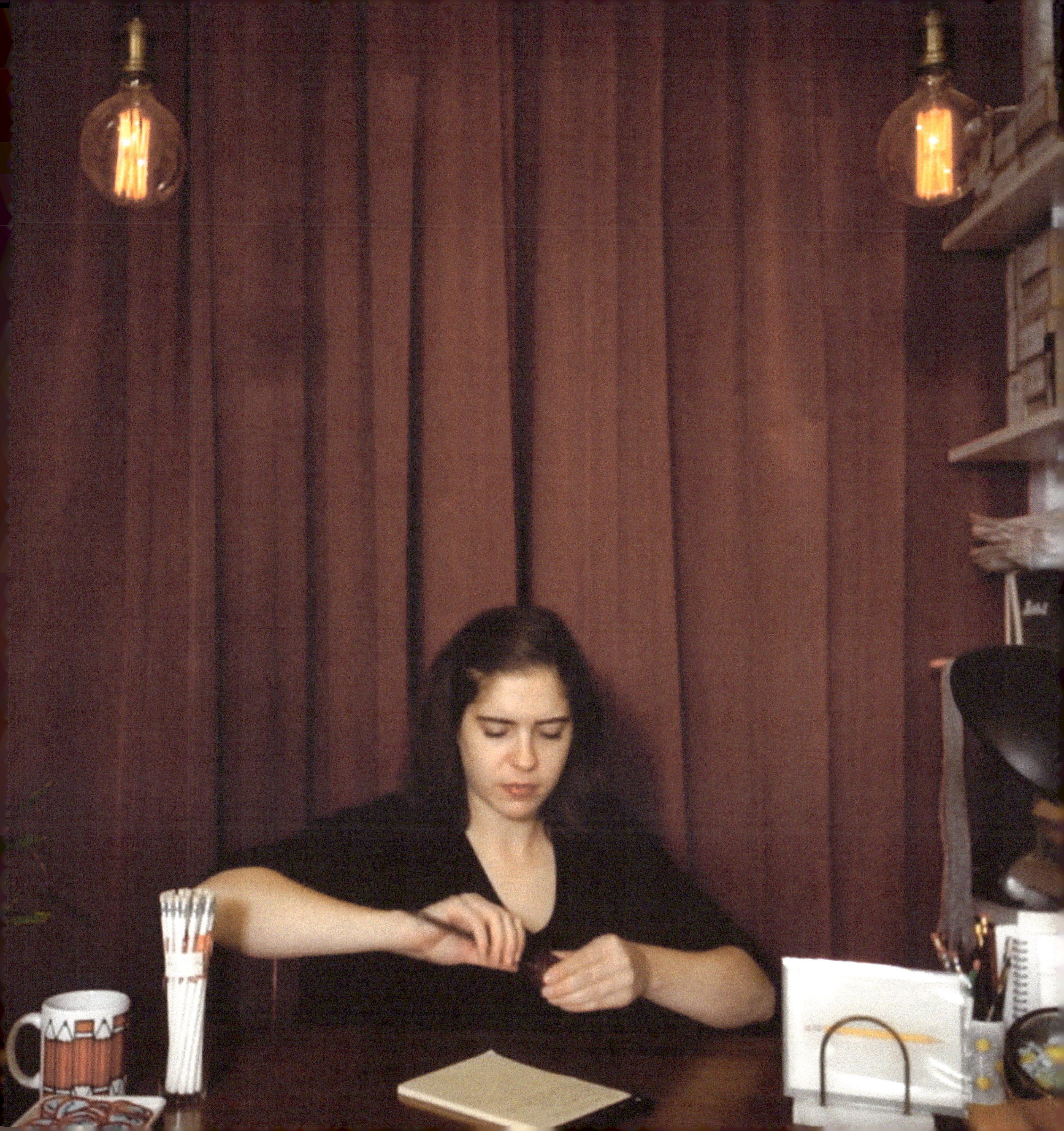

I think there is a pencil revolution happening. With all these advancements in technology, especially in the younger generations, like kids my age, they are really getting into analog gadgets because it's no longer really a necessity. Things like pencils are something that are almost a novelty these days.

It's a rediscover of how pleasurable physical things can be and they get a little hooked, but not in a way that one would with something that is an essential item on your desk. They act like using a pencil is a treat, a thing you do when you don't have to use a computer. That's what I think is really great about what's happening right now, this kind of resurgence of analog tools.

Memories of the Pencil

My earliest memory with a pencil was from when I was about six years old. My mother went on a trip to Italy and brought back a set of Caran d'Ache colored pencils that came in the most beautiful tin that had wildflowers on the cover. It was eighteen perfect pencils, all lined up in color order. I didn't want to use them because they were just too pretty. I grew up in rural Ohio, where all we really had was a Wal-Mart and an Office Max about twenty miles away. I had just never seen anything like it.

Then she borrowed them when she was working on her scrapbooking and lost them for about ten years, eventually finding them in the back of her desk. I remember being so excited that these things were rediscovered because I had just had it as a fantasy in my head that I used to have these colored pencils that were so beautiful. I still have them. I still use them. I have taken them with me everywhere I've ever lived.

Selecting a Pencil

If you are a newbie pencil enthusiast, you should just try one of each, or ask and I'll suggest my favorites. I have pretty standard pencil taste. I feel like most people agree with me when I pick out my favorites, but I think if you're new to pencils, you kind of have to decide what you like about them first. You have to decide if it matters that there's an eraser, or if you're left-handed, or if you like a scratchy pencil or a really smooth pencil. Some people really like the sound that comes with writing with a pencil, and some people don't want to hear that at all, so it depends on what you're looking for. You have to establish what the basic rules are for choosing a pencil before you are able to figure out what your pencil is.

Left-Handed Pencils

A lot of people are left-handed, and they generally hate writing with a pencil because it smudges. The thing is, if you're left-handed, when it comes to a pencil, you're generally looking for something that is dark and smooth but not smudgy. A lot of Japanese pencils tend to satisfy that because Japanese pencils, in general, have a quality of being really smooth and dark without being as smudgy, but left-handed people feel like they can't use pencils, or they feel like they have to use super light or super hard pencils, which isn't fair. It makes me sad. I really want all left-handed people to know that there is a pencil for them.

Victory Lap

It's hard to determine how a pencil can stand out in a society, like we live in now, where technology generally rules everything. Because the thing about pencils is that there's not a lot of new technology when it comes to them. Things haven't really changed when it comes to how pencils are made, and I'm not sure that it will. I'm really not sure that it has to, either.

With a pencil, there's a reason why it has existed for so long and why it still exists. There's a reason why, first of all, it took so long to come up with the modern

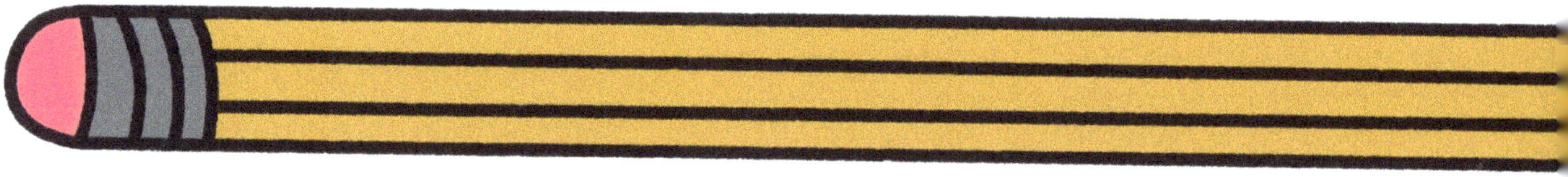

pencil. It took decades upon decades to design a way to make the pencil as we know it now. For the pencil moving forward, it has more to do with marketing. Pencil brands need to step up their game and market pencils as something that is still useful in a person's daily life, something that is cool, looks nice, and has a place on your desk in a pencil cup, in whatever capacity that may be.

Missing

I think a world without a pencil is not a world I want to live in, but I also think a world without a pencil would be a pretty sad place. A world without pencils would be drastically different. People's brains would work differently because there's not that physical connection. I don't even want to think about what it would be like if we didn't write by hand. It's a really good brain exercise and something that's really good physically and mentally. Let's hope that doesn't happen. Let's make that not happen.

Writing with a pencil is really freeing because, first of all, it erases. People are a lot more willing when it comes to writing with a pencil as opposed to a pen. They don't think so much about it.
They just kind of go.

Because pencils are so tactile, there are so many kinds of sensory factors about writing with a pencil—the smell, the sound, the feeling of wearing a pencil down and having to sharpen it again, the mess you make when you use an eraser. Those sorts of things

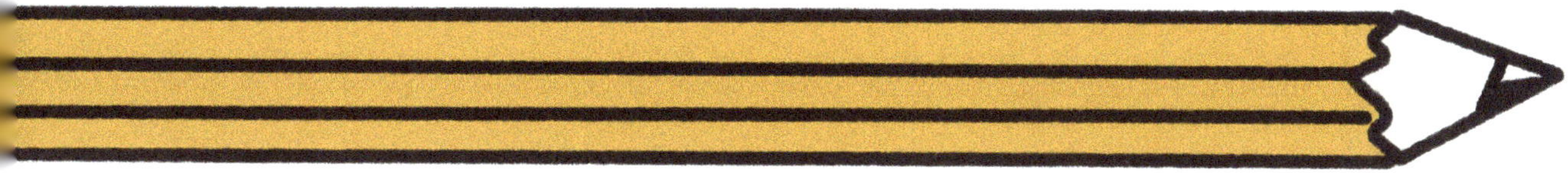

make it a physical experience, even though all you're doing is putting graphite on a piece of paper. That's a really important aspect to realize and to recognize when you're using a pencil.

Greatness

To me, what makes a pencil great is the feeling of writing with it more than anything else, more than what it looks like, more than where it comes from. I want to write with it and feel really excited about writing with it. I want to feel like I want to write more, not like I just need to get through my list or get through whatever I'm doing. To me, a perfect pencil smells like cedar, but isn't overwhelming. A perfect pencil is smooth but not smudgy, dark but not overwhelmingly so. I like pencils with a slightly longer point.

I don't use erasers. I prefer to just mark things out. I want to be able to see my mistakes. I want to remember what I had written and decided I didn't want to write anymore.

I enjoy all pencils for different reasons. I don't really have a favorite pencil. I don't love one type of pencil more than another. I think they all have their place, but I just want to really feel like I'm doing something when I'm writing with a pencil.

Technological Battle

If I were a pencil in this day and age, I would be really stubborn. I would be kind of mad about the fact that all these other modes of writing think they are better than me. I would be an old-fashioned, bitter pencil. I'd probably feel elitist. I'd probably be a bit angry.

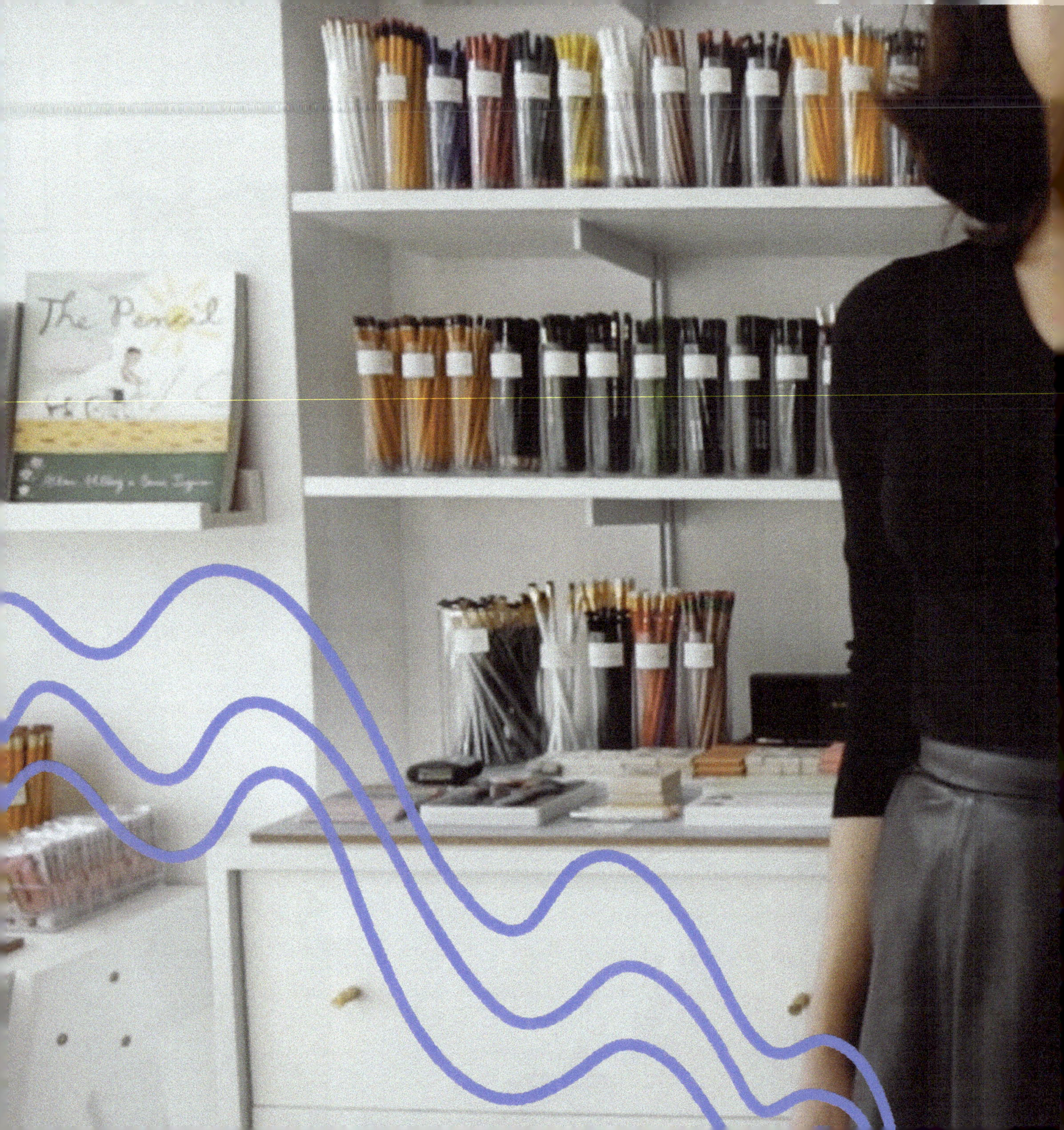

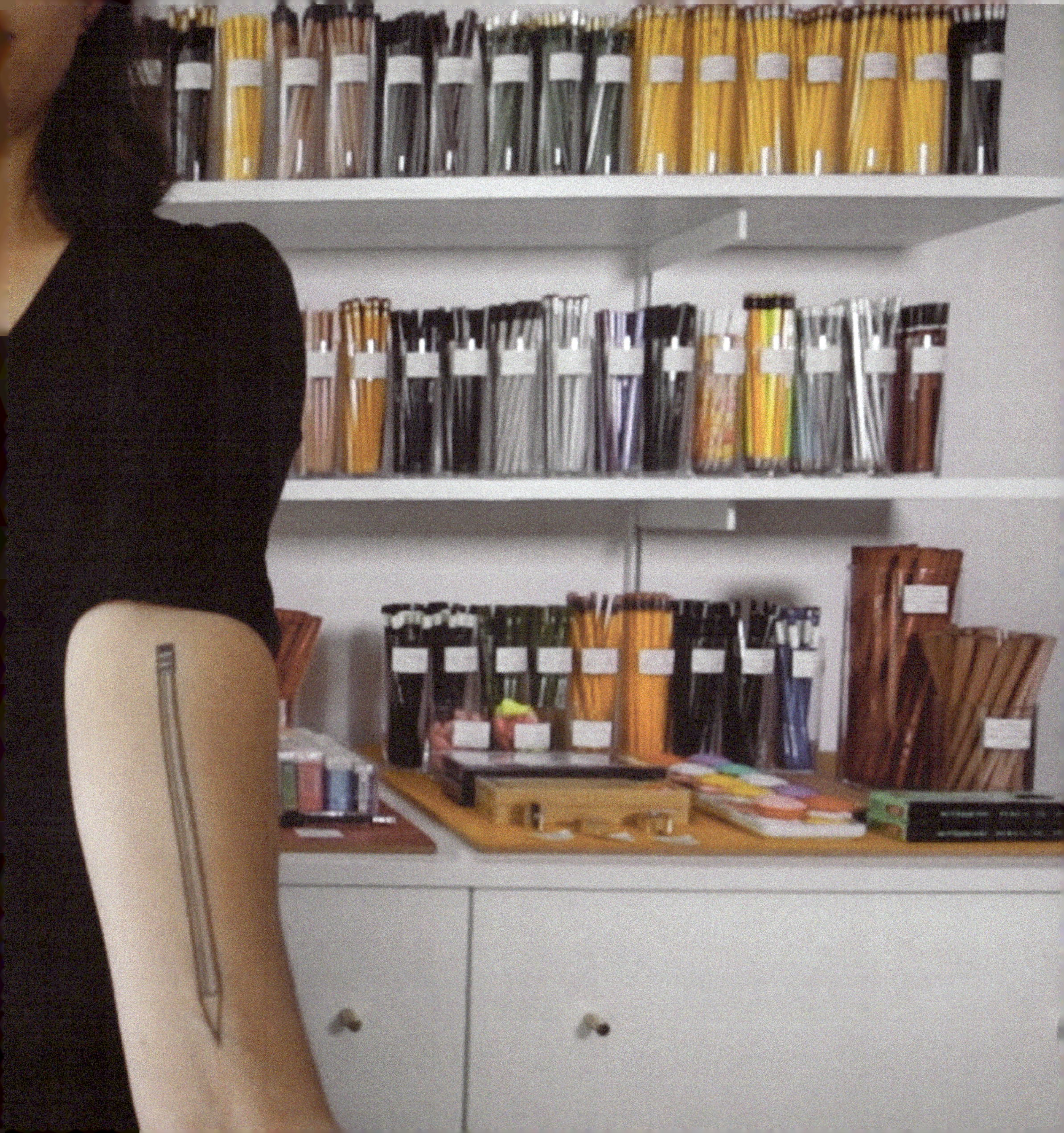

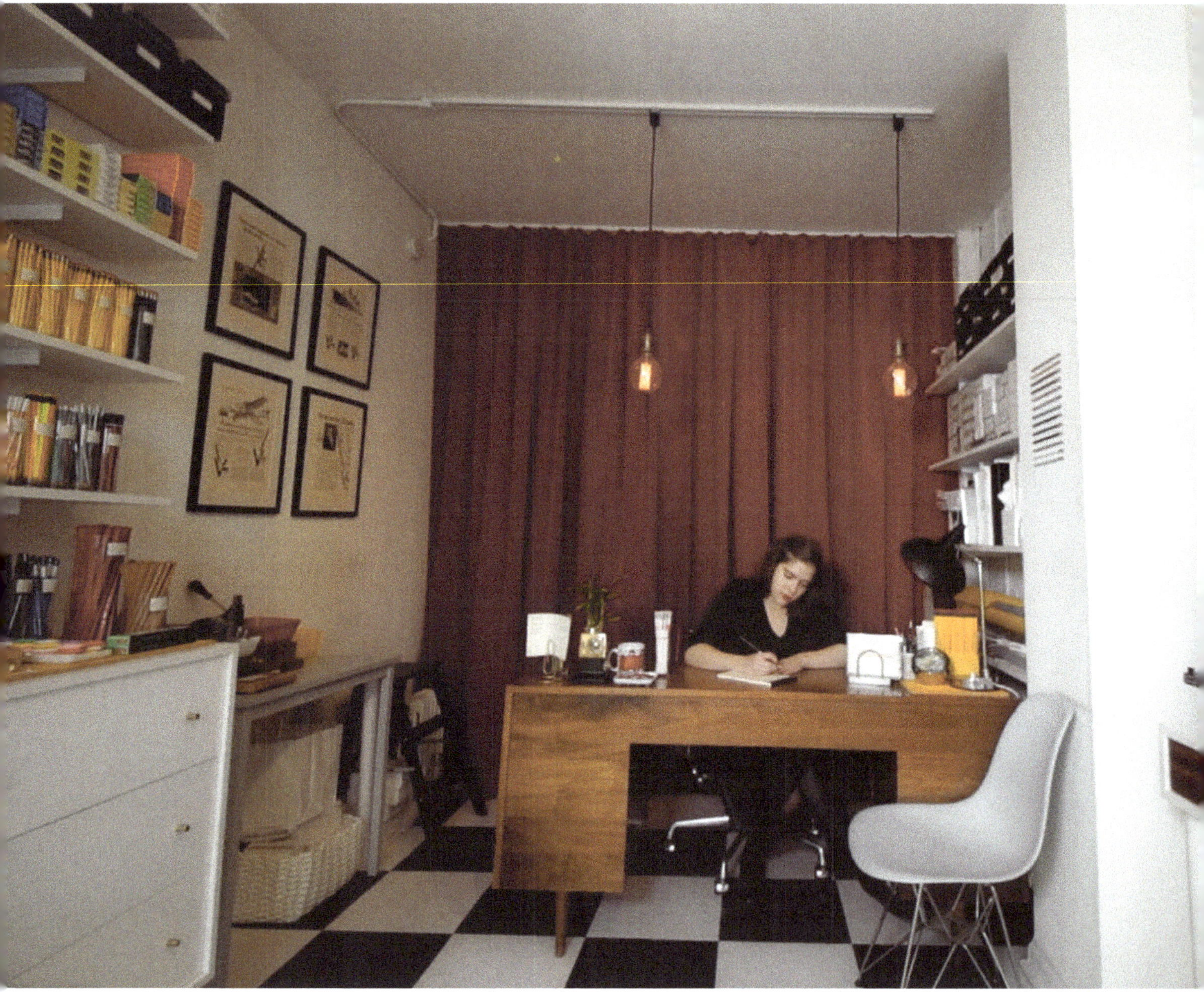

But maybe a pencil doesn't have to be angry. Maybe if I were a pencil, I would be really stubborn. I would want people to still believe that technology can't beat me, and maybe it can't. I would just want people to remember that I'm pretty awesome, too, and that you can't just replace me. You can't replace pencils. It's not going to happen. If I were a pencil, no computer could do what I do.

I think there is a pencil revolution happening right now, that the more advanced we get with technology, the more people crave analog writing and other older fascinations. They treat it more as a novelty and less as a necessity. It's fun to use your hands, to actually do something with them besides typing. People want to do it because it's pleasurable, it's nice, and it's physical. It's not typing. It may not be something that people need to do every day, but it's something people want to do more and more. For that reason, it's making a comeback.

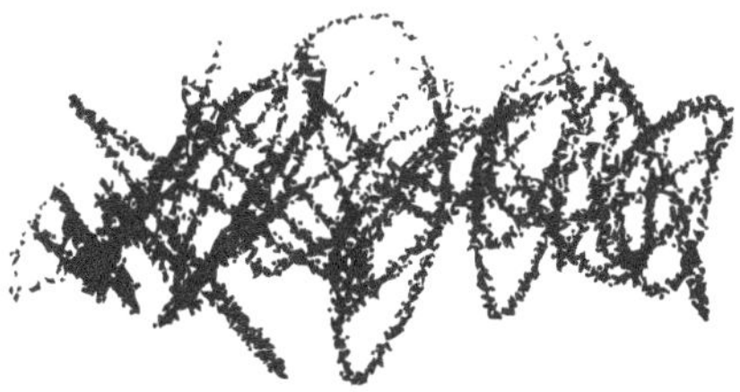

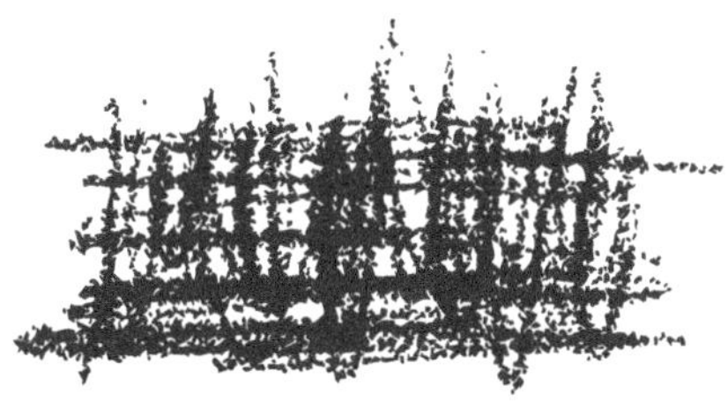

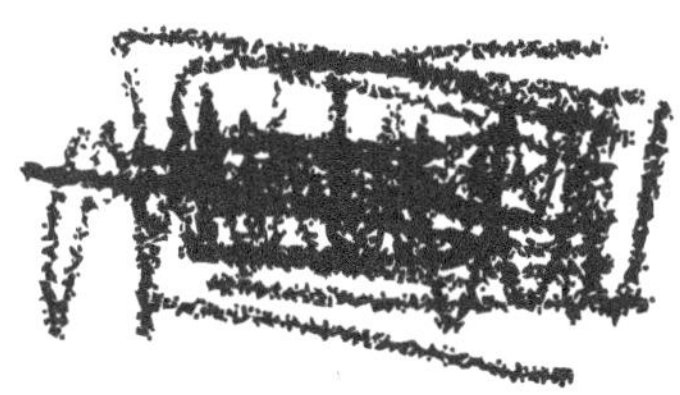

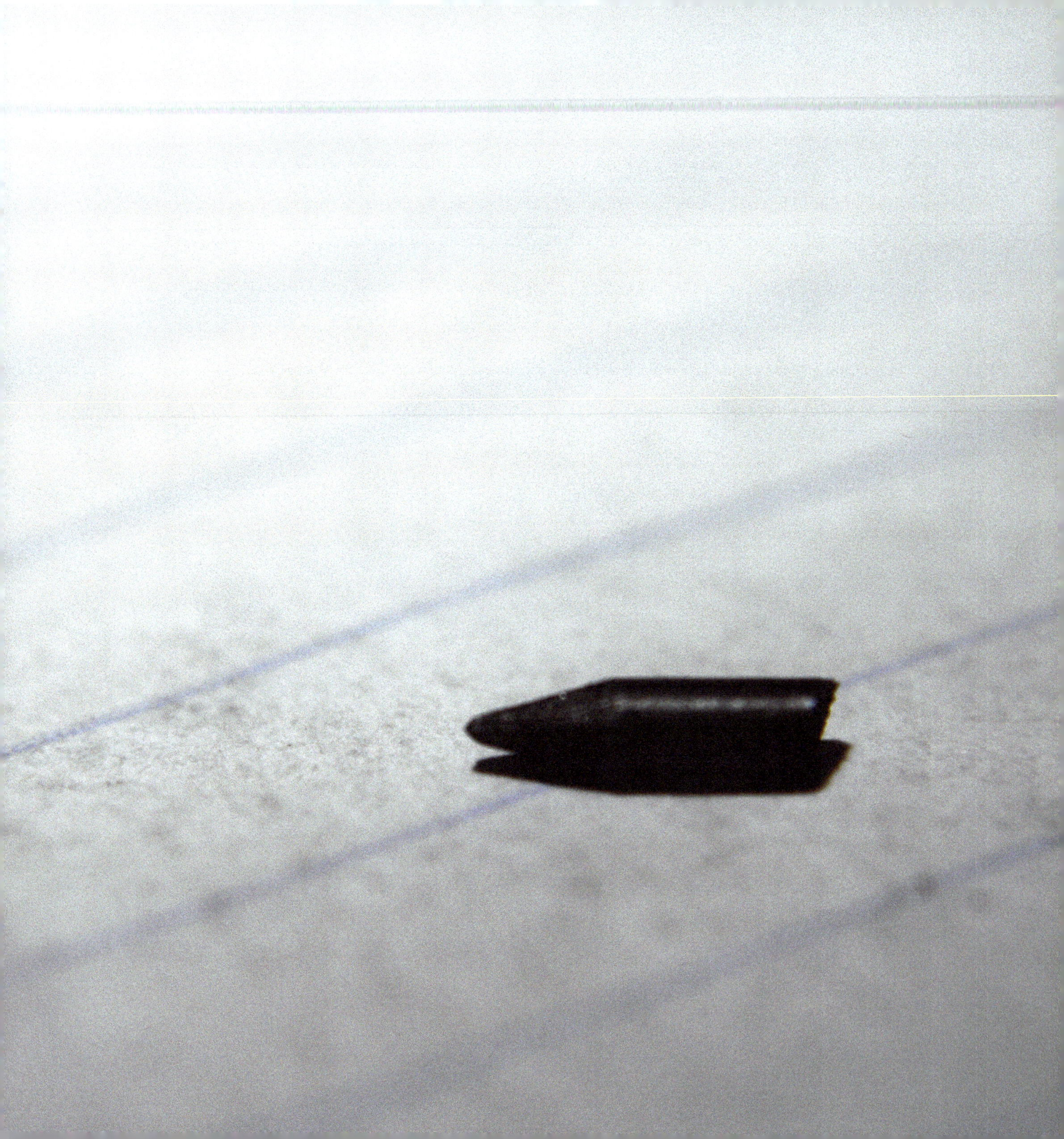

Emphasis

artistic technique focusing attention on a specific element or area

The Original Blackwing 602

Sean Malone

"Gone but not forgotten"

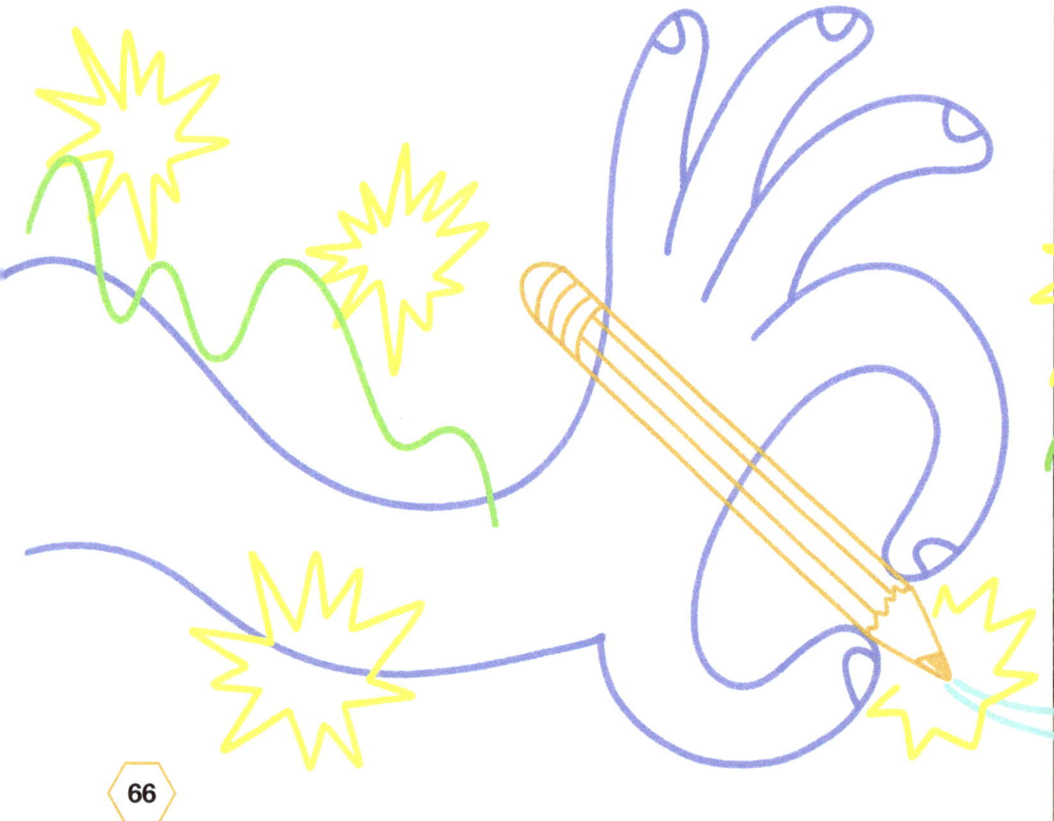

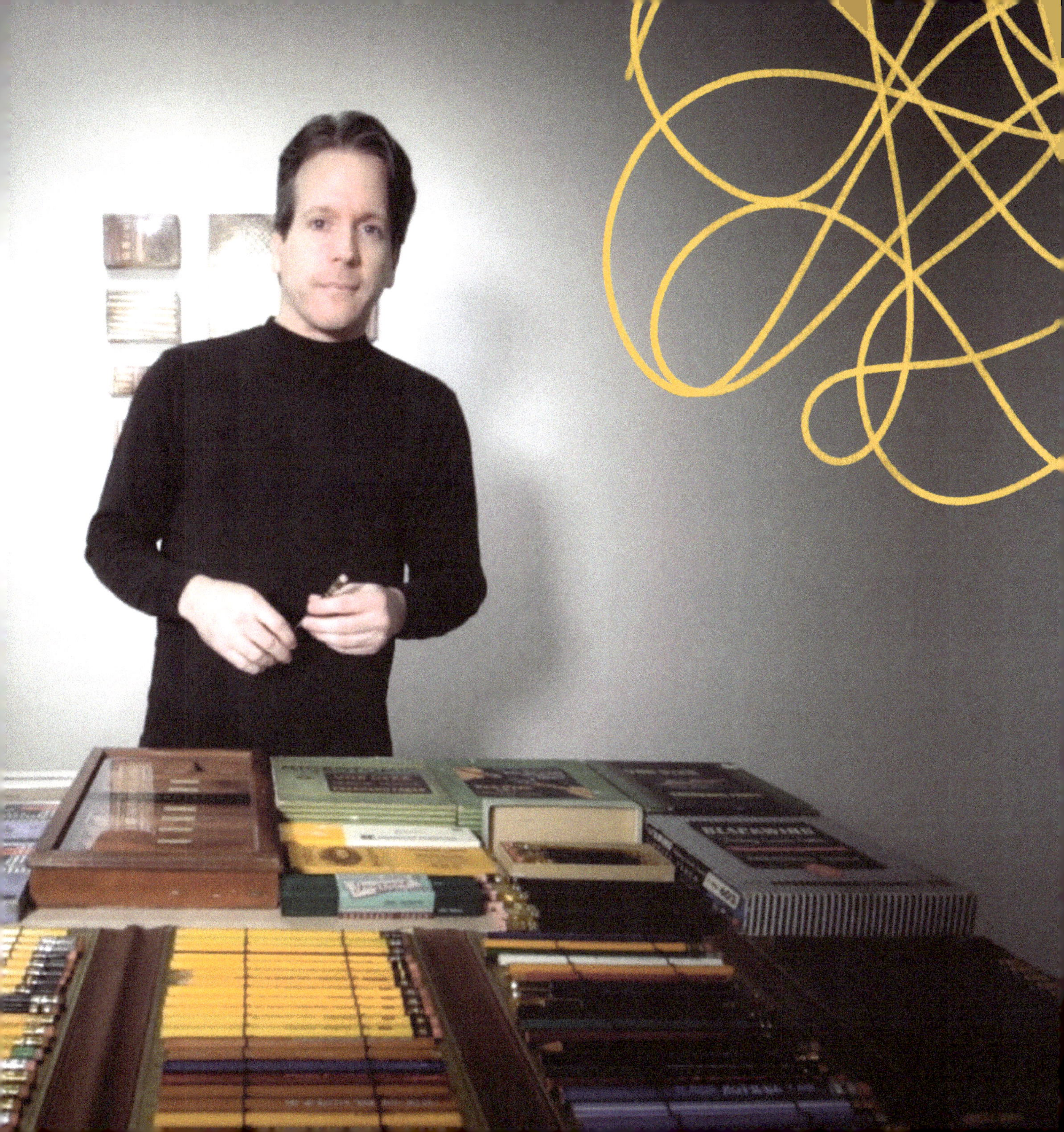

What pencil to use may seem trivial to most people, but when it's a big part of your creative output, it's important what pencil you use. That's one of the most interesting aspects to the 602. When you see one, especially with the eraser and the form of it, because it looks a bit different, that may further drive an interest in it. Plus, they're difficult to find, and when you do find them, they're often extraordinarily costly and prohibitively expensive to even use. But when you do get a chance to write with one, you notice there is something different about it. It's something you may have never experienced before, and so that's enough to get somebody hooked. That's pretty much what got me hooked.

When you first see a Blackwing pencil, you might see it has an unusual shape to it, something you're not used to seeing. Then, when you finally get a chance to write with one, that's what will usually hook you. That's what hooked me when I finally got to try one.

When you pick up a Blackwing 602 and write with it, one thing that you can expect is your physical experience isn't going to be similar to ones you've had before. If you're not used to trying different kinds of pencils, that is. If you're used to using soft lead pencils, perhaps it'll be a familiar experience, except for the fact that, as soft as it feels, the point doesn't wear down in the fashion you'd expect. That's the allure—it's so smooth and waxy feeling, but you have the point retention, more like the number 2 pencil. It's not a dark pencil, either, so all of those things make it almost counter-intuitive when you go to write with it. You think certain things are going to happen, but it seems like the opposite happens. I had one friend say that it felt like it was writing by itself, which is an excellent compliment for a pencil.

Interest in the 602

One of the things that got me interested in the 602's history was seeing how many people had been using it in the past. There are some famous names that come up quickly, such as Sondheim and Steinbeck, but once you start looking (and sometimes it's just a search through photos on the internet), you'll see Igor Stravinsky using one.

I'm a musician, so I look first to musicians. That got me wondering: was there an ad campaign? How did they know about this pencil in an age when things weren't advertised in the same way they are advertised today? How many different kinds of disciplines? People who were cartoonists and animators, writers, all these different disciplines were using and wanting this same pencil.

Another thing that was interesting to me is that it seemed to be by word of mouth. I like the fact that it seemed to be less about a big advertising budget than it was, "Hey, I heard from so and so that this is a great pencil. You should try this. This pencil really works nicely." I saw pictures of Wynton Marsalis using one in a 1998 picture. For musicians and artists, the 602s are tools of the trade. It's what they talk about.

How Many 602s are There?

How many original 602s are out there is difficult to say. I remember an email conversation with a friend where I said the Blackwing was a rare pencil. He replied, "I don't know how rare it is." I thought to myself, Well, of course, it's rare. He went on to say, "Well, no, it's hard to find, but that doesn't mean they're necessarily rare, so there could be vast stores of these things in places." It's hard to know, but interestingly, most people who are going after them are people who want to use them. So, every day, there's at least one less Blackwing in the world. The numbers are only getting smaller.

Shelf Life of a Pencil

"What future does the pencil have?" I told him that I think the pencil is the future. Count Anton Faber-

Castell, in Germany, mentioned once that if you put a pencil in a drawer, leave it for a hundred years, come back to it, pick it up and, first stroke, it's going to work. There are not a lot of writing instruments that can still say that. It's like an instant time machine with the pencil.

Revolution

It's sad the way handwriting is not being taught in schools the way it once was, but you have to cede to technology. But because of technology, you don't have to use that technology, so we're the people for whom writing matters, and the comfort and natural feel of something. The pencil is always going to be around and be useful. I just hope that companies can survive long enough to keep producing the high-quality pencils they're looking for.

For me, with the Blackwing, it started when I finally got one and thought, Well, I just spent this money on it, so I'm not going to sharpen it. But of course, I did.

I eventually got a few more and noticed that the

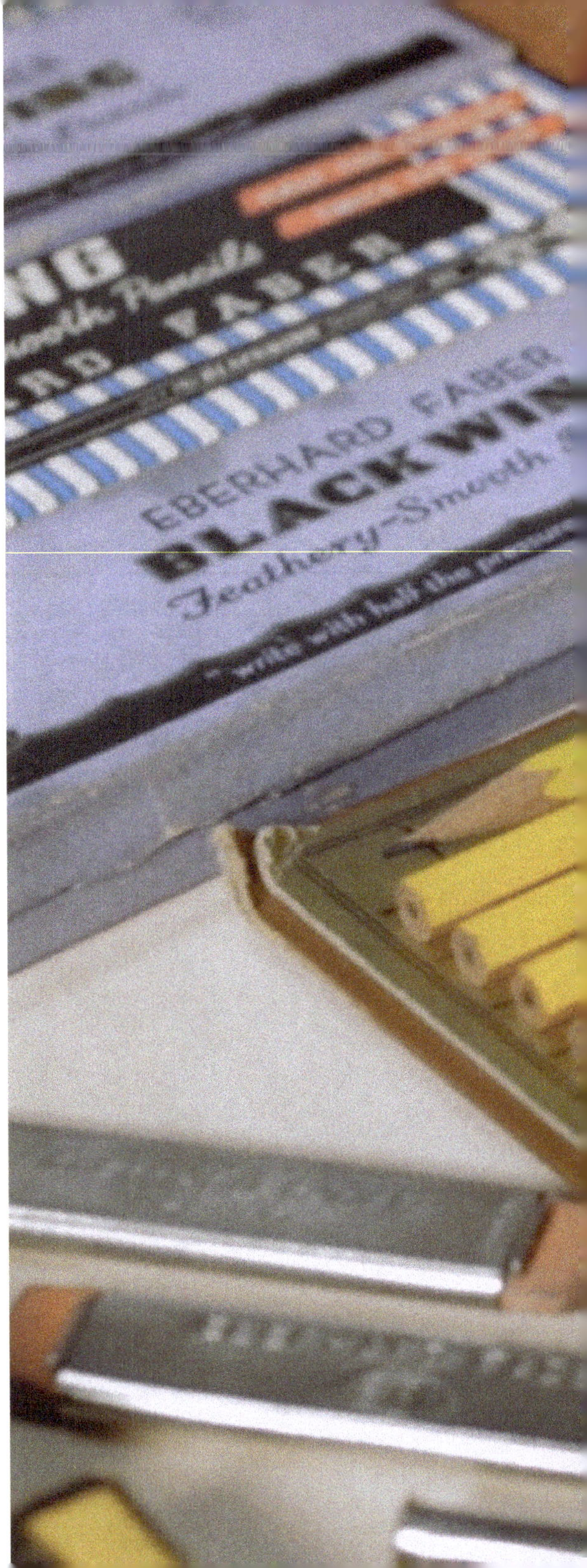

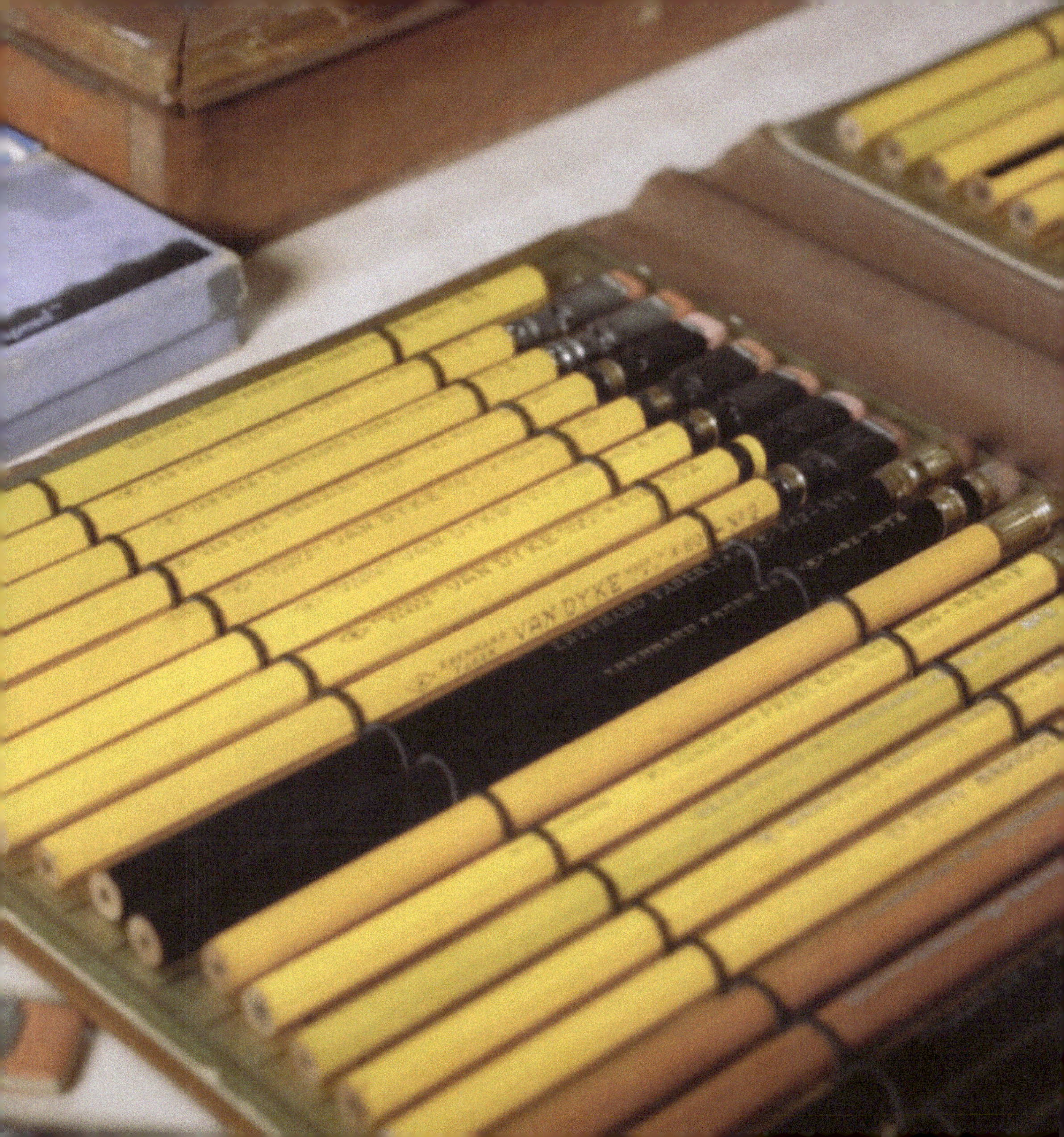
VAN DYKE

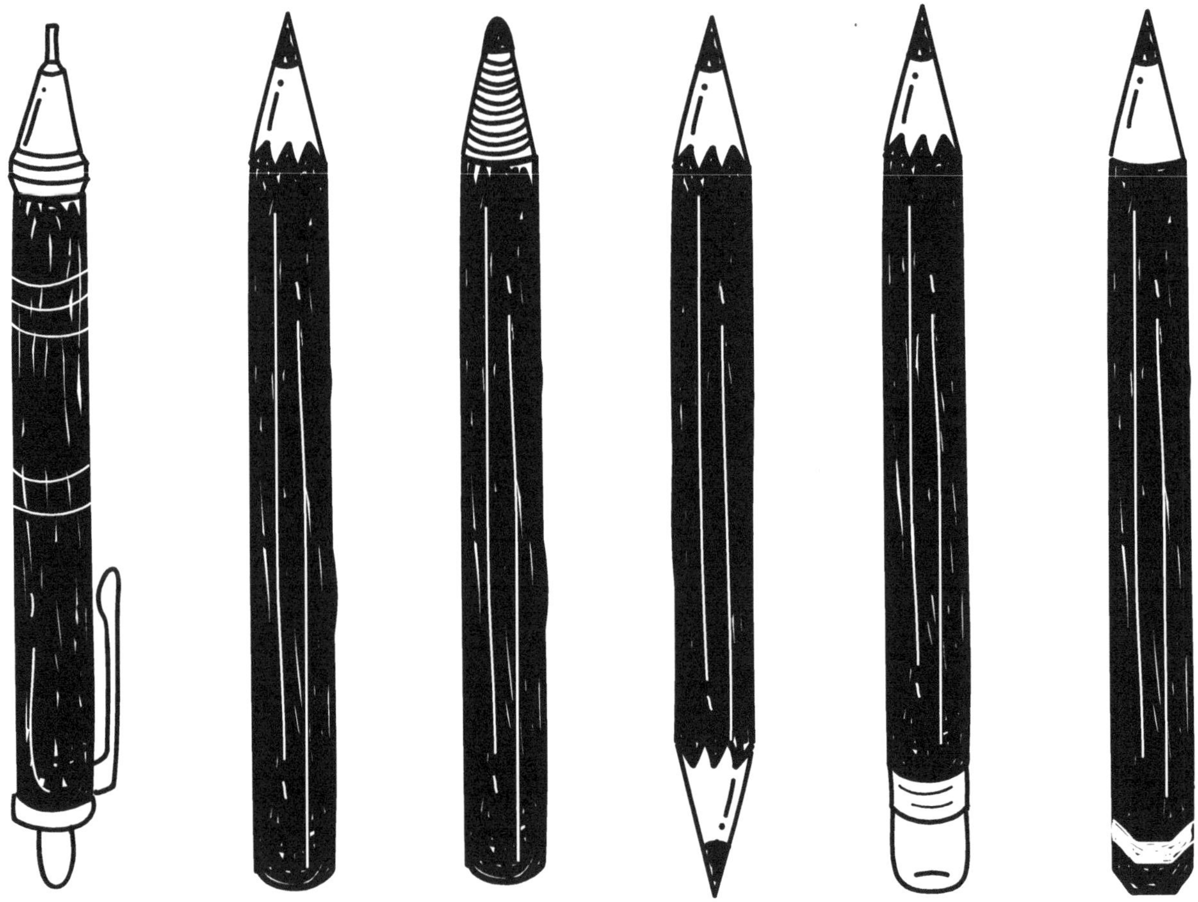

imprint was different on each of them. It got me wondering, Why would it change? I can understand if you want to freshen something up, but there were five different pencils, and each of them had something distinctly different about it.

I started looking around online to discover there's nothing to be found about it. In fact, it's difficult to find information on the history of pencils in general. It's usually just the same story about how pencils started over in England then developed into modern pencils.

Collection

I don't fetishize my pencils. I try to take care of them and show them to people who are interested in seeing them. When I say I have a small collection, I think anyone who saw it would say, "That's not a small collection." But when you talk to pencil collectors, these are people who have on order tens of thousands of pencils, and even more than that. I stuck to a small, narrowed group of manufacturers.

For me, there has been so many pencils made just by those companies that the idea of trying to track one down of each of them is a several lifetimes' pursuit. Well, unless you can get your hands on one, maybe from an estate sale, a really good starter collection or something like that. I try to take care of them and, like I said, sharpen and use most of them, to the horror of my collector friends. Other than that, I do like to keep at least one good example of each pencil to make sure I have one that lasts.

Uniqueness

When someone writes with a Blackwing 602 for the first time, the first thing they'll notice is that the shape of it is a little bit different. Of course, it looks like a normal pencil with a barrel, but the clamp eraser design, which was patented in 1921, is adjustable. It was one of the first pencils with an adjustable eraser, which was a pretty neat idea to begin with. Then they used this design on several other pencils. Almost every single time I've handed a 602 to someone to start writing with, the first thing they do is look at it, as if to say, "That didn't seem right" or "Something felt off about that. That's not how a pencil normally writes." That's the first experience most people have with it.

After Midnight

One of the things that got me interested in the history of American pencil making was the fact that it seemed to have disappeared almost overnight in the late 80s and early 90s. There were so many manufacturers for so long, including the Eberhart Faber company, which had been around since 1849.

When you take a look at some old catalogs, some old advertisements, you see just the breadth of products they manufactured, the quality, the innovation that went into them. That goes for all the other companies, but especially with Eberhart Faber that I became interested in.

To think that it would disappear within a generation, or even half a generation, was sad. I think it had something to do with the fact that we're losing our touch with handwriting, the fact that pencils don't hold the same position they once did. At the same time, it's something that ought to be remembered. I think it's important. It's one of the largest and first corporations in America. It has a long family history, going back to Germany, as well. The history of the Eberhart Faber company is something to know and understand.

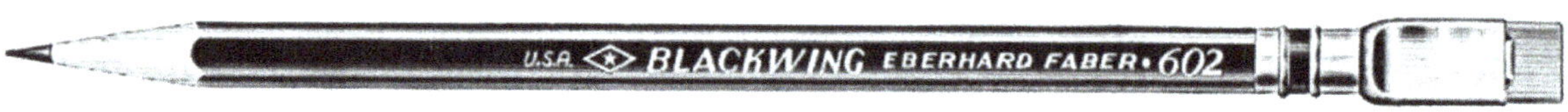

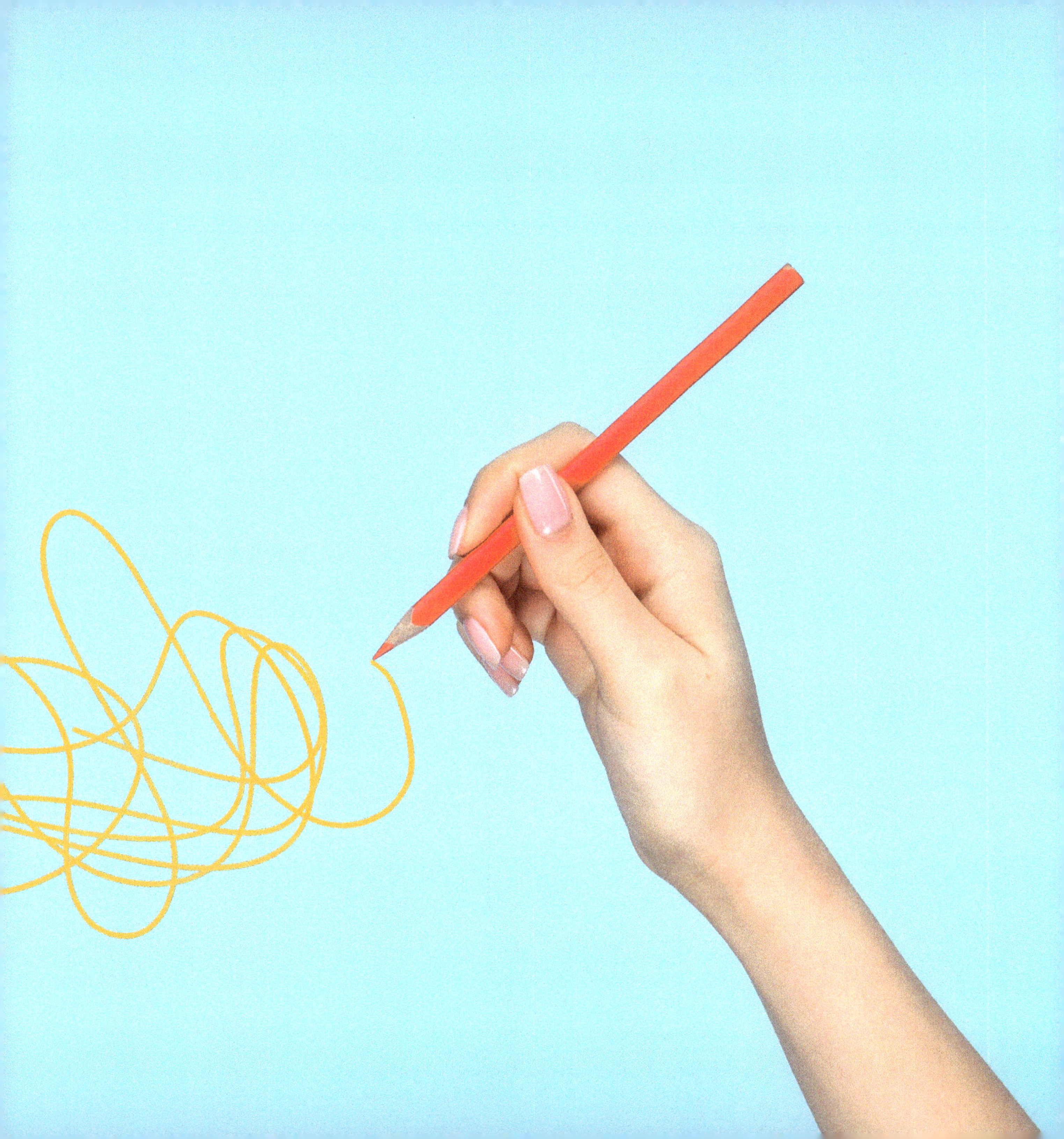

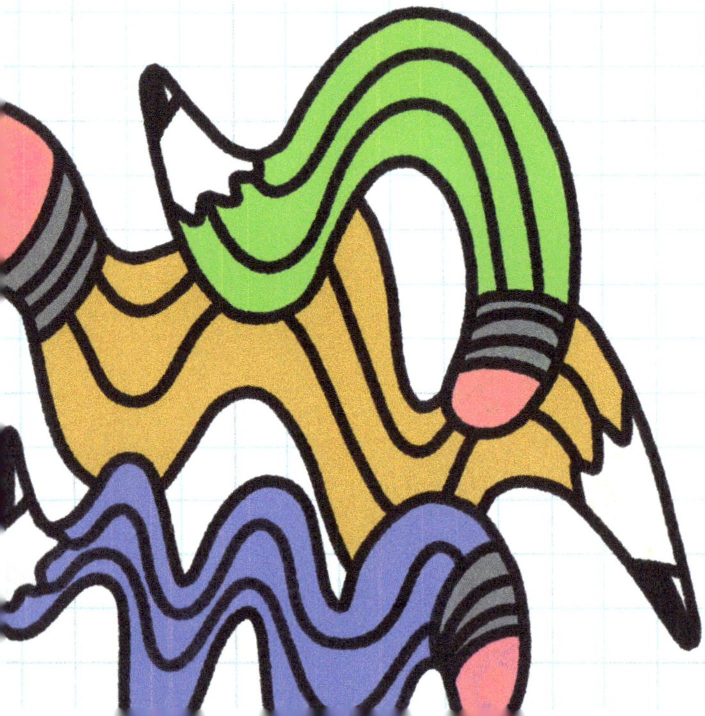

Ideas

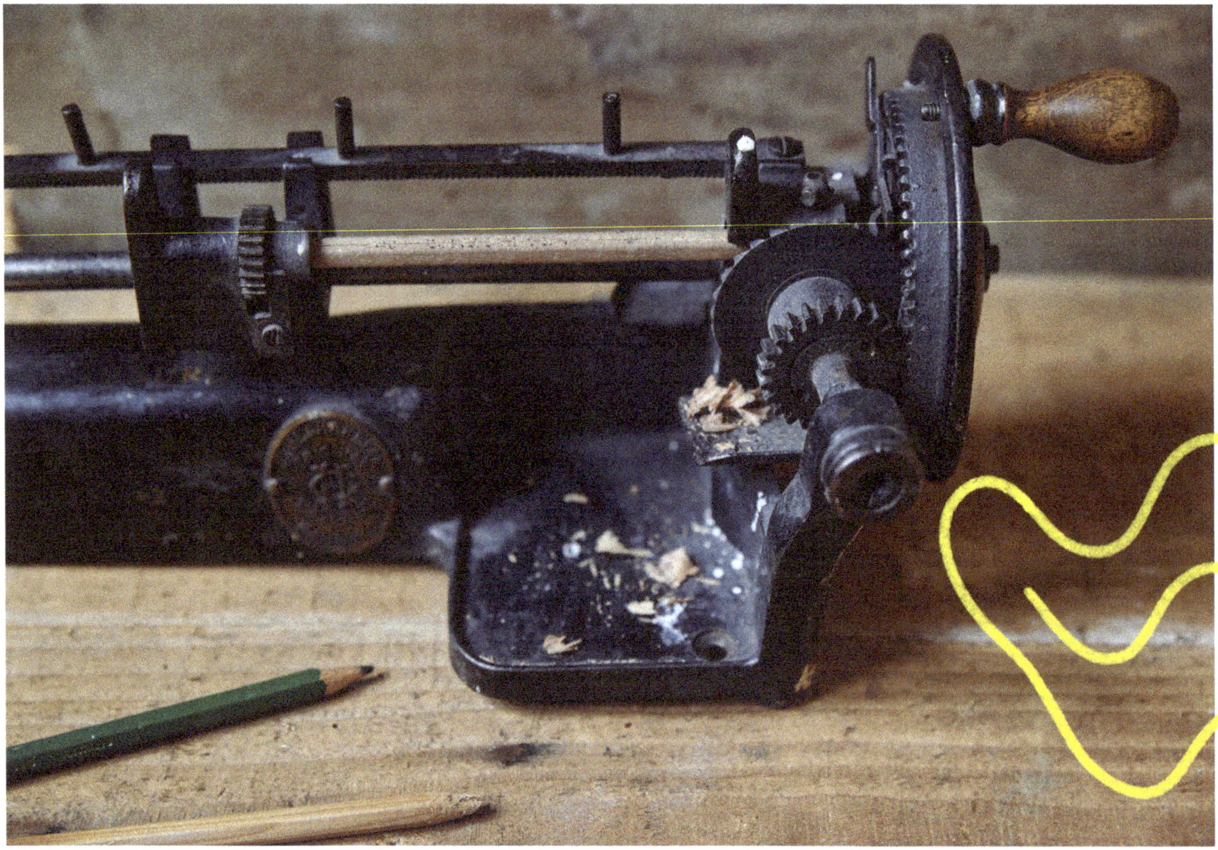

Pencil Sharpening

David Rees, Author of How to Sharpen Pencils

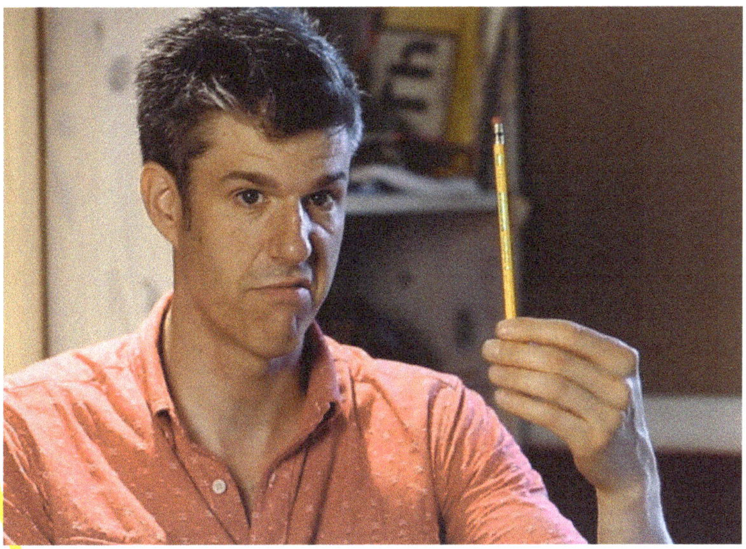

On that day of staff training at the Census office, we were all standing around the trash can, sharpening our pencils, the shavings coming out, and I was like, "I'm doing a good job here. I'll put my pencil up against any of these other Census employees' pencils." What would happen if I really started applying myself to this practice? So, I think that's when I knew. And that's when I thought, You know, there's got to be a way where I can figure out how to get paid to sharpen pencils.

Adulthood

My early memories of pencils were in elementary school, going to the school store in the hallway and buying new pencils, new graph paper, new erasers. This is why kids love learning how to sharpen pencils. When you're a kid, a pencil is a sophisticated, adult-like tool. And sharpening it is good for kids because it shows mastery of fine motor skills. You're taking this object and putting a point on it, which means now you can use it like a real grownup.

I remember buying school supplies and loving them. They were brand new. Like the night before the first day of school, my mom would take me to the store to get a brand new notebook, brand new notebook paper, brand new pencils, and we would just lay it all out on our bedspread and be like, "I'm so grown up right now." I remember the associations I had with them. For me, they're nostalgic.

The New New Medium

If kids stopped using pencils, I don't think the world would end, but kids should definitely learn how to write by hand, because the thought that attends that process is different than the type of thinking you do when you're typing on a keyboard.

I'm someone who often writes by hand, because I'm

a slow writer. I feel like I have to hold my thoughts back until I'm done with one thought, and then release the next one, so I can write it down. Whereas I'm actually a pretty fast typist. But I do think there is a lot to writing by hand.

I would be bummed out if everything went digital in classrooms. Plus, this whole idea that if everyone gets a free laptop, that that's going to solve all education problems in this country, is techno utopianism, which I can't stand.

The Beauty of the Pencil

There are a bunch of ways to look at a pencil. You can look at it as an engineering tool, like an object that represents centuries of experimentation and innovation. In that regard, what's remarkable is its efficiency and utility. It has no moving parts. You turn the pencil into a moving part. There aren't many components—the eraser, the ferrule, the barrel, and then inside the barrel is the graphite. But the composition of the graphite took a long time to get right, and people still experiment with that. The glue that binds the graphite to the barrel is a whole other kettle of fish. The quality of the eraser is a big deal. And as an engineered object, there are pencils of greater or lesser quality.

Pencils from a hundred years ago would blow away the pencils that are easier to buy in America today, because they are usually made abroad, out of cheap wood. They're produced with a mind for keeping costs as low as possible. But I've talked to plenty of teachers who say, "What is it about today's pencils? They are inferior. I remember pencils being well made. These pencils are horrible. The graphite breaks off in the sharpener. The graphite isn't centered within the barrel." There are a bunch of issues with pencils.

And again, one of the remarkable things about it is an incredibly low-cost, effective, basically permanent, robust communication tool that you can literally buy for pennies and use for years, if you know how to use it correctly. And you can write something that will be read, theoretically, centuries from now. Even beyond that, if you want to zoom out even more from thinking about it as a communication tool, you can think about it as a metaphorical object.

Metaphorical

The pencil is still the iconic symbol for communication, especially among kids and people in academia. Idea communication, back of the envelope calculations, or a rough draft of a painting or something—all these things we associate with pencils, because the pencil can be erased, which is a pretty heavy metaphorical state of affairs.

On the same tool, you have one end that is the creation side, and then, literally on the other end of it, you have the negation of that. It's like the alpha and the omega on this little yellow stick.

I think pencils and pens each have their advantages and disadvantages, and so do typewriters and word processors. But when it comes to just a really compact, powerful, metaphorically potent object, the pencil crushes all those other communication tools.

This has literally been winnowed down to the essentials of communication and, in a way, human experience—creation, advancement, negation, erasure. I think that's why I'm kind of fascinated with them—for the different ways you can look at it: as an object, as a symbol of communication, and then as a symbol of something even greater, like the symbol of the human experience.

Deity

For me, it was like a weird form of pencil evangelism. I am skeptical of people assuming technology is going to solve all of our problems, or that a new, shiny technological device will mean we don't need to address fundamental issues about education and class, or whatever.

And so, in a way, I wanted to use the pencil to celebrate not just analog technology, but also when you think about the pencil as an engineering device that was designed for accessible communication, it blows an iPad out of the water. It's so much more

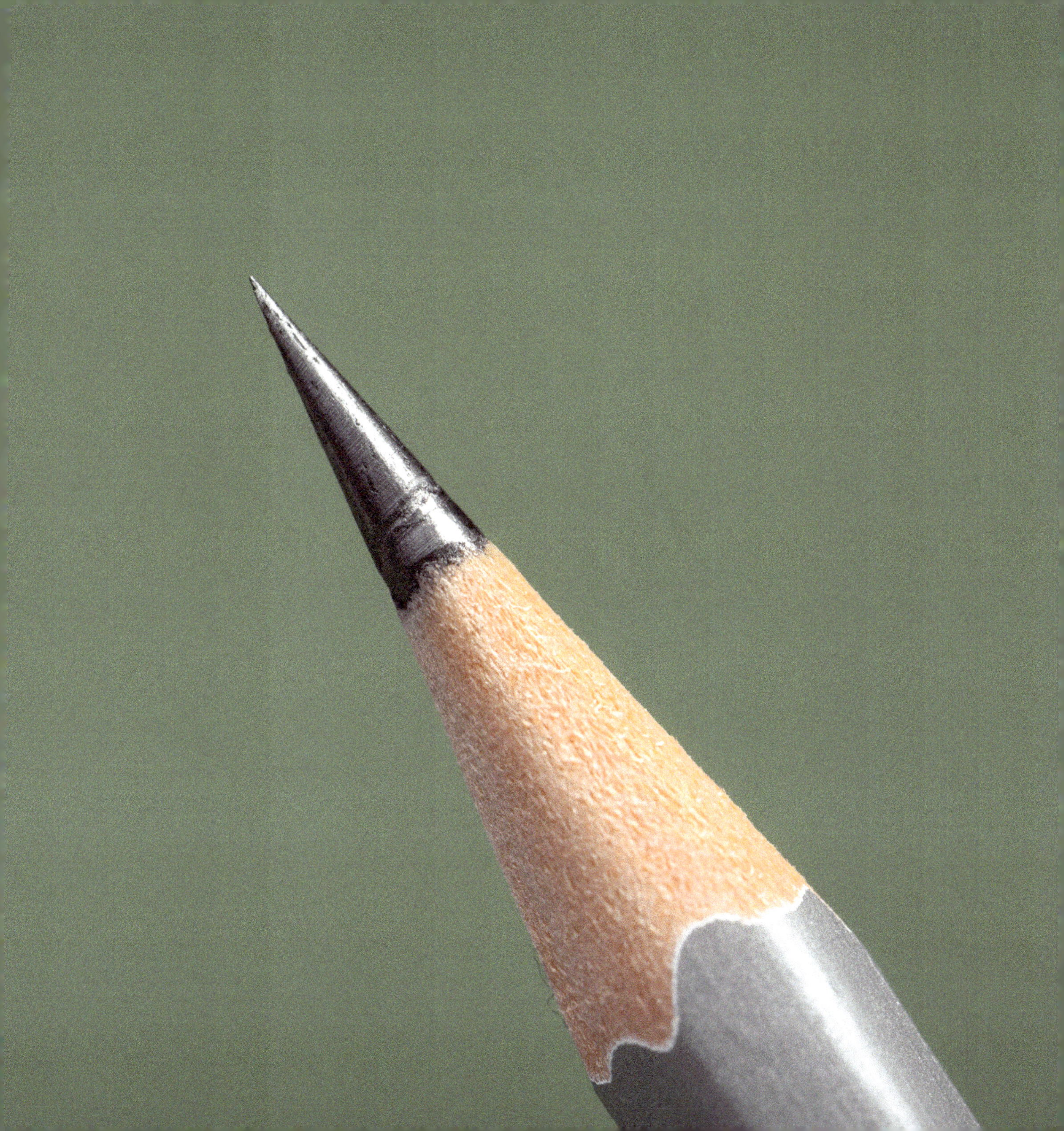

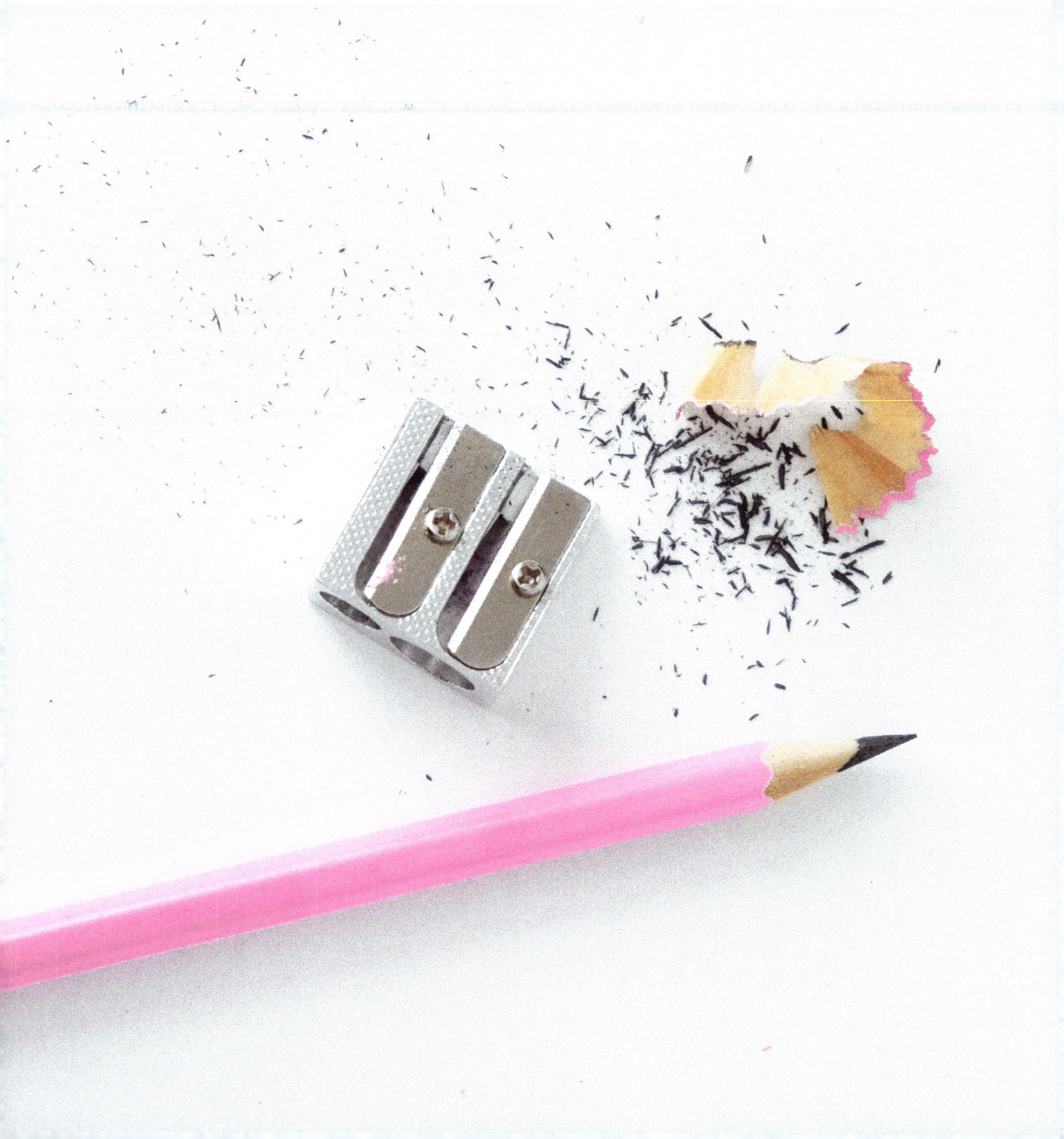

impressive than anything Steve Jobs ever came up with. And it's so effective, efficient, and ubiquitous that it does become something we take for granted and never think about unless like, "Oh, I got to write that down. Let me find a pencil." You pull open your drawer, and there's like six thousand half-sharpened, chewed-up pencils, which is a testament to just how beautifully designed it is. It's probably the one communication tool that is in every house in America. There's a lot of pencils out in the world, and each one is special.

You can have a fancy iPad, or iPod, or something, but the pencil is twenty times more amazing.

Celebrate

It's about celebrating the things that we take for granted and don't think about. We live in a society, especially in a consumer culture, that commands we celebrate and salivate over whatever the newest product is. That keeps the engines of capitalism moving forward, which is fine. On the other hand, if that comes at the expense of neglecting the things that have been around us our whole life, to the point where we can no longer even see how amazing they are, I think that's a shame.

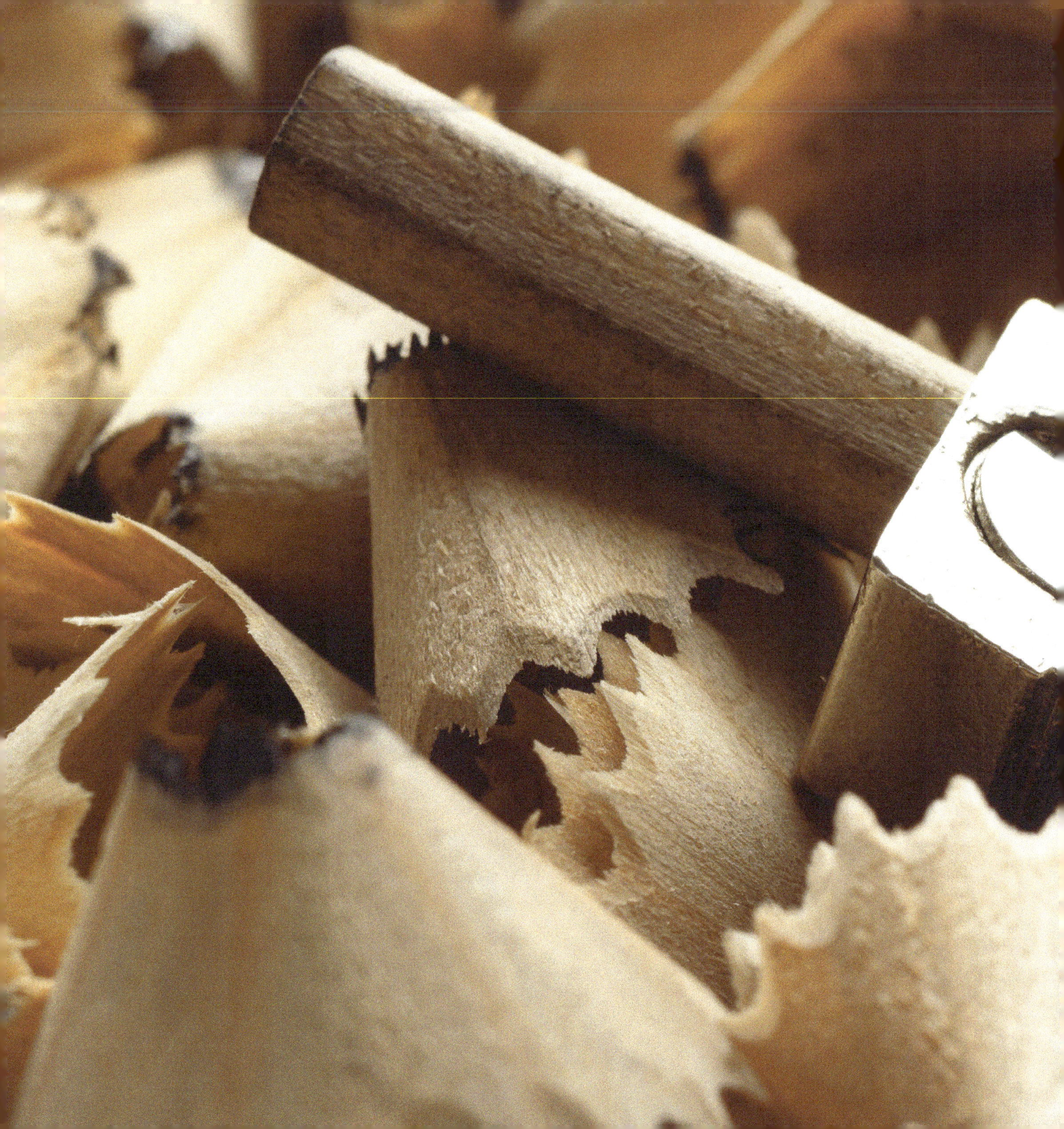

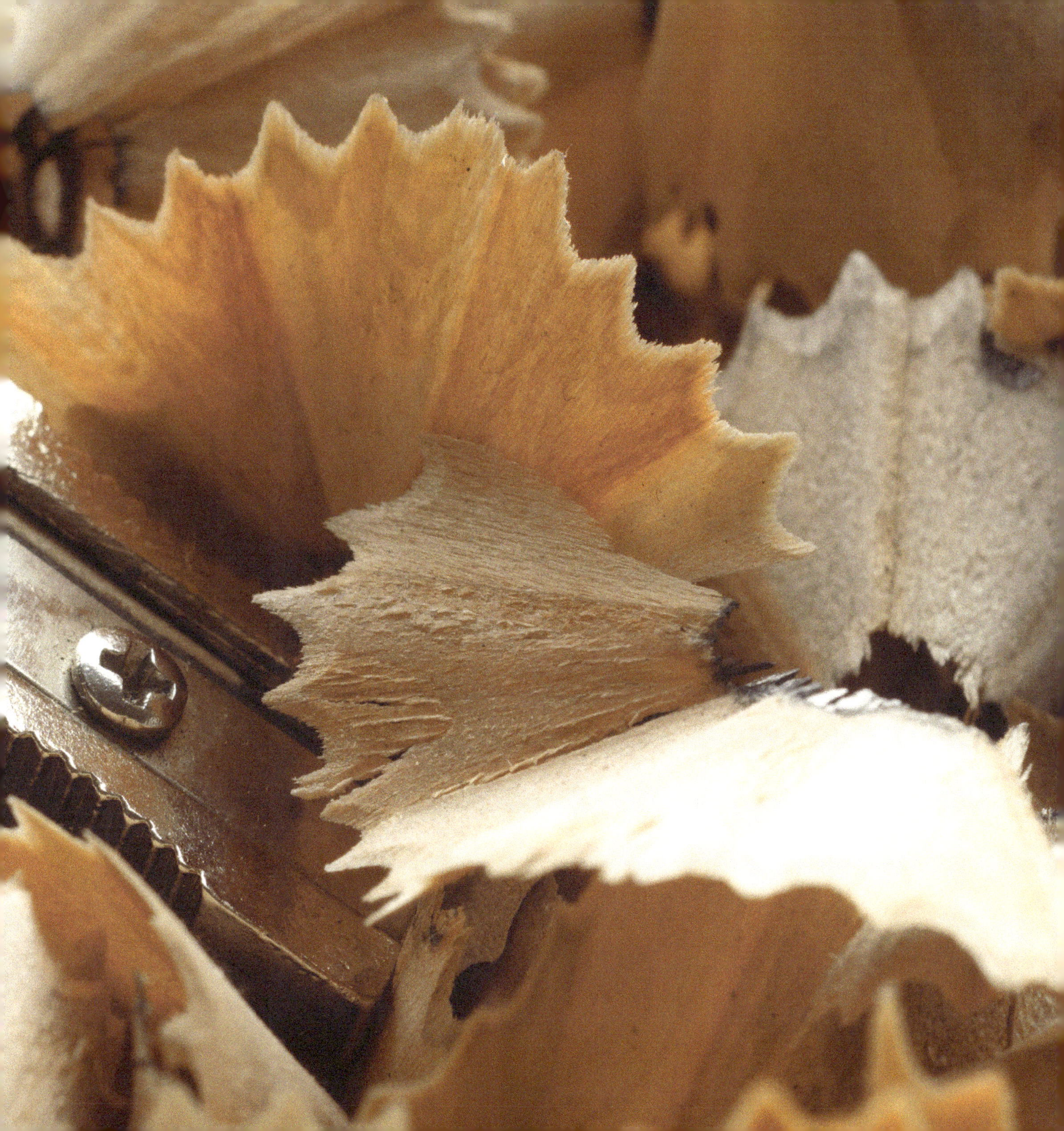

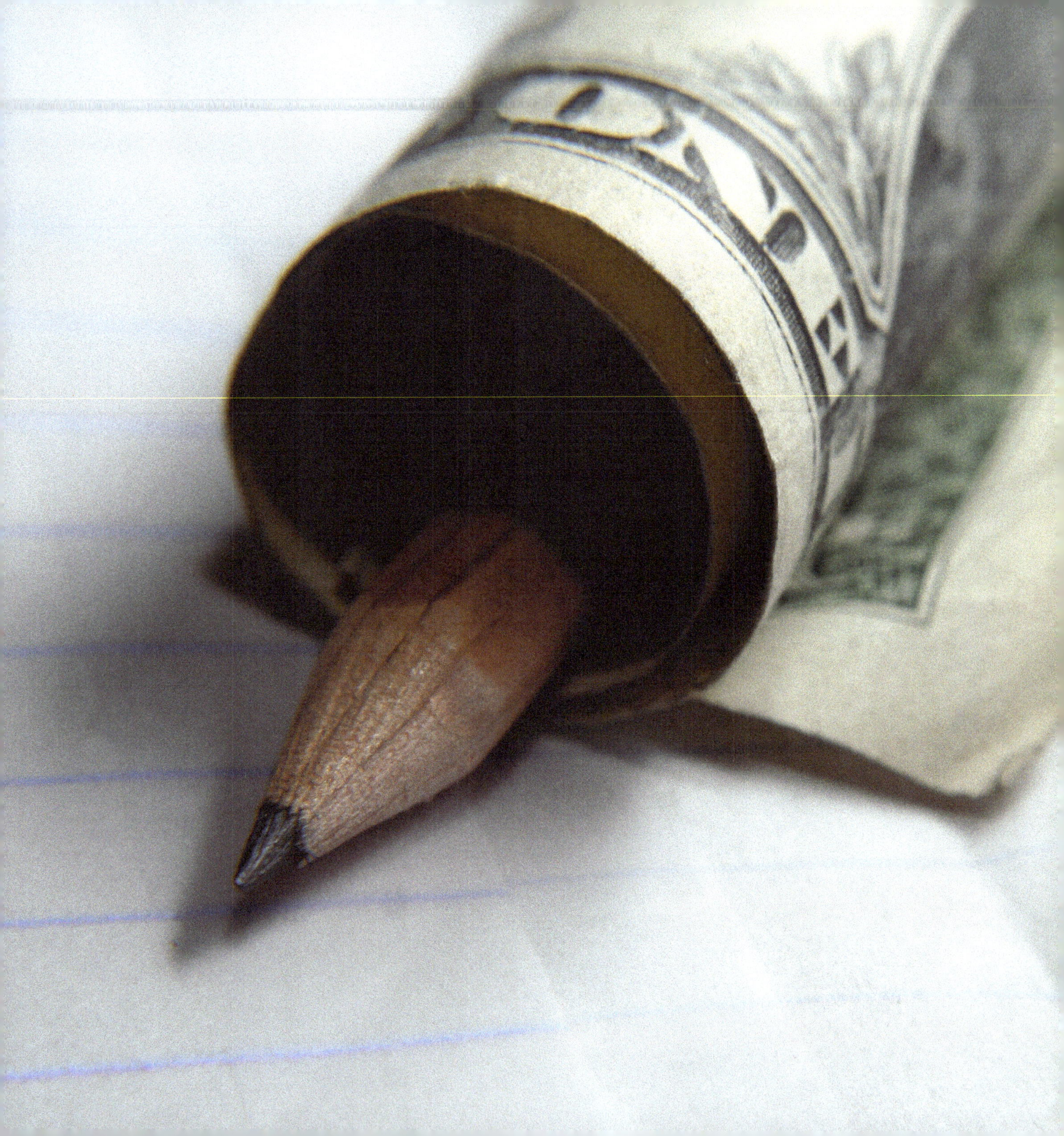

Value

perceived lightness or darkness of colors and shades in artwork

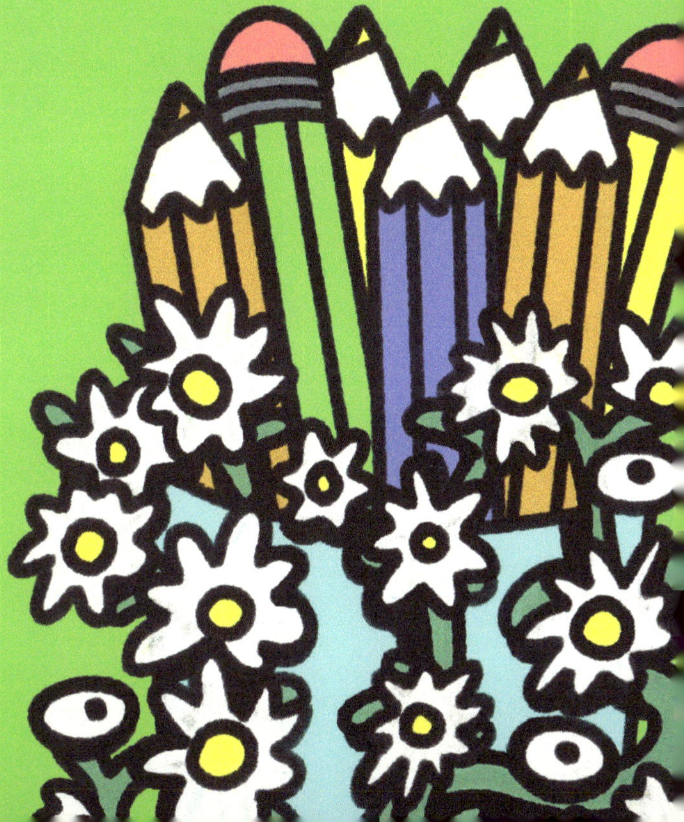

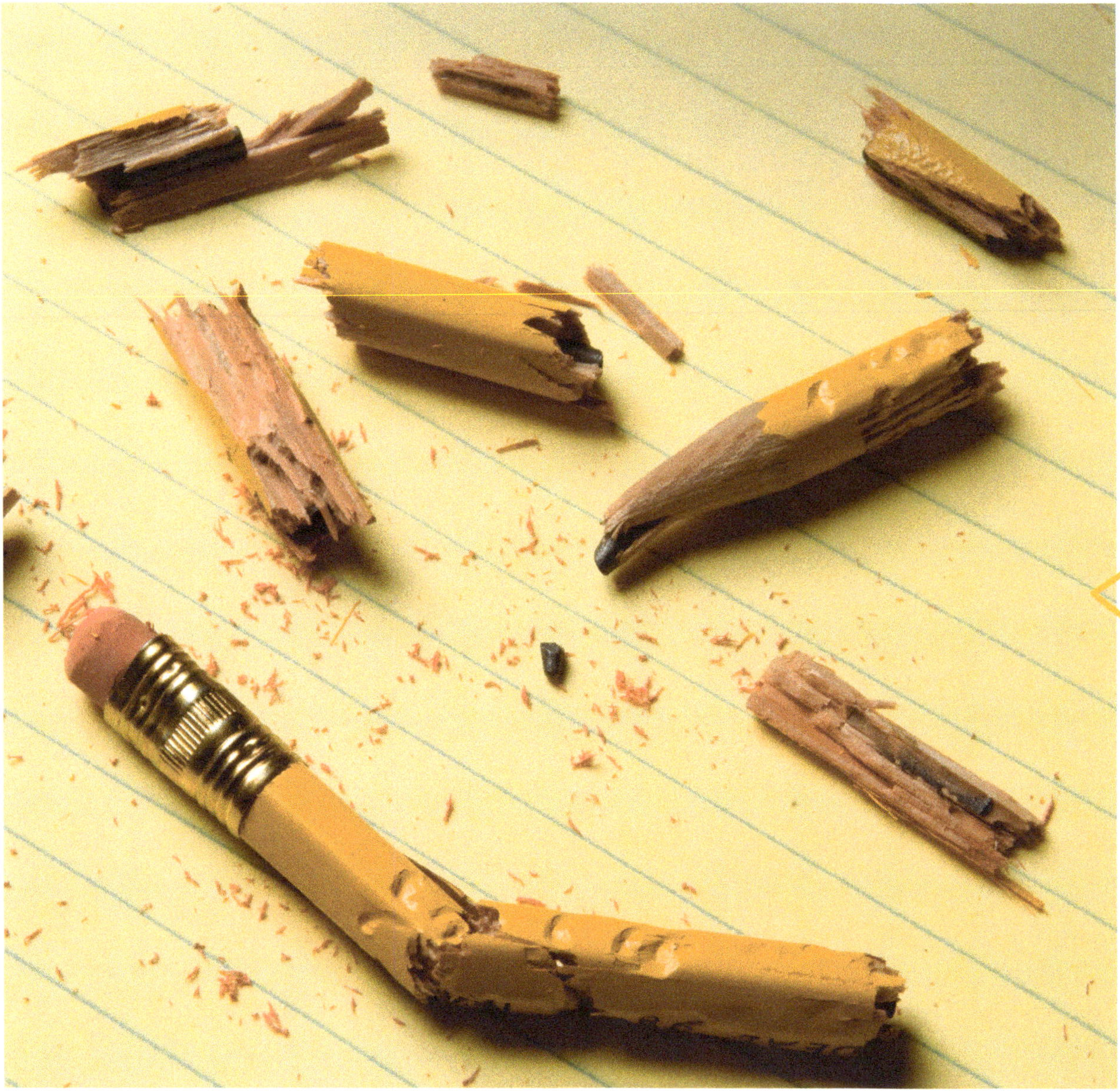

Without a Soul

Raphael Esquer, Principal/Graphic Designer-
Alfalfa Studios, NYC

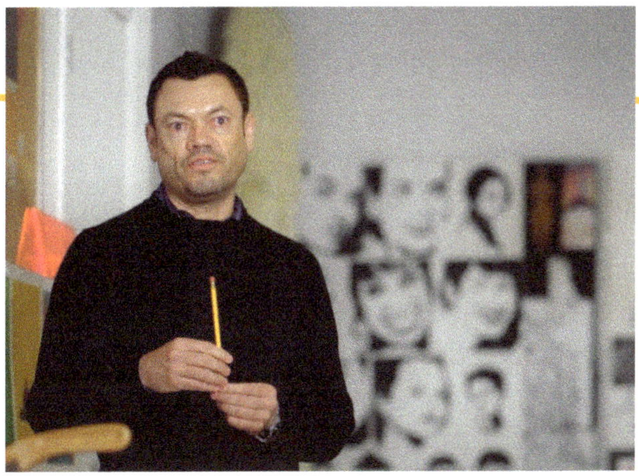

If I was a pencil, would I worry about technology? I don't think I would worry too much. Technology comes and goes, things come, go, and fade. And throughout the evolution, I think the pencil's been around for hundreds of years, and it will be around for hundreds of years more. In a few decades, computers will be a thing of the past, or they will be evolved too much. Things as basic as a pencil will stay around, for sure.

My Work with the Pencil

One thing that connects my work with myself is the pencil. Without it, it would be without a soul. I see a lot of work and a lot of design that is created directly in technology like computers. It's lacking that heart, that humanity. For my work, having to sketch everything by pencil, by hand, before you go into production, just makes a difference.

After the research, once you've filled your mind with ideas, I sketch to execute and actually sketch a lot. From those sketches, then becomes the process of elimination. Once I'm sure that this is the idea that I want to create, then I use whatever production tools available to make it happen. I never jump onto a computer without having a clear idea from a sketch that was created beforehand.

In my creative process, sketching is a really big part. After I do the research and really get to know the subject, then comes this delicious process of sketching. It's where ideas come. It's the connection between your mind and the paper, literally through a pencil. I actually have sketchbooks from the last twenty years that are filled with drawings. So, a lot of the work that has been produced has started there. That was the genesis.

I think skipping the pencil phase in my work, or the work that was created, would be unspirited or without a soul. I see a lot of design work that was created directly on the computer, and you can see that it's just maybe too perfect, done almost by a machine.

In my case, starting with a pencil sketch just makes the work more alive, more rich, with more layers of feelings.

Why?

Why should we use the pencil today? It's still relevant. First of all, it's inexpensive, I don't think it ever fails, and all you need is this thing and whatever piece of paper to use. Write down your ideas, or draw them in my case. I can see it used in every single profession—mathematician, a gardener, a writer. Just even with this, you still see people in the street to this day, and it's more present than any other laptop or electronic.

Benefits

Art is manifested in so many different ways. A lot of artists—most all—have a sketchbook. In the sketchbook, are pencil drawings. Maybe there is a collage, some cut and paste stuff, but the genesis of ideas come in sketchbooks. I've been doing it myself for the last twenty-something years. A lot of the work you see starts there. I like to think that artists have a similar approach.

Innovation

I think the way the pencil has remained has innovated the way I use it. I can see the evolution, since I don't use it the same way as when I was younger. It was just a thing to make a line. Then, as you keep getting familiar with it, you start discovering the shading and the amount of pressure you put on the pencil and the paper. It just changes the character. It's getting familiar with the tool and discovering all the possibilities that something so simple can give you. Professionally, I think that the work I do stands out because you can see a process. You can see some soul in the work. It starts with this.

Forgotten

The question is: do I think new technology coming out copying the original is beneficial? I think it's a compliment. They want to be it, but it's an imitation. Nothing beats the original. I think it's great that all of these things are coming up and probably making work faster, more efficient. Again, I think starting with the pencil works better for me.

The worst-case scenario for a pencil is the worst-case scenario for a lot of things—to be forgotten. It has been replaced in some ways, but I don't know if it will get to that point where it gets forgotten, not anytime soon, anyway.

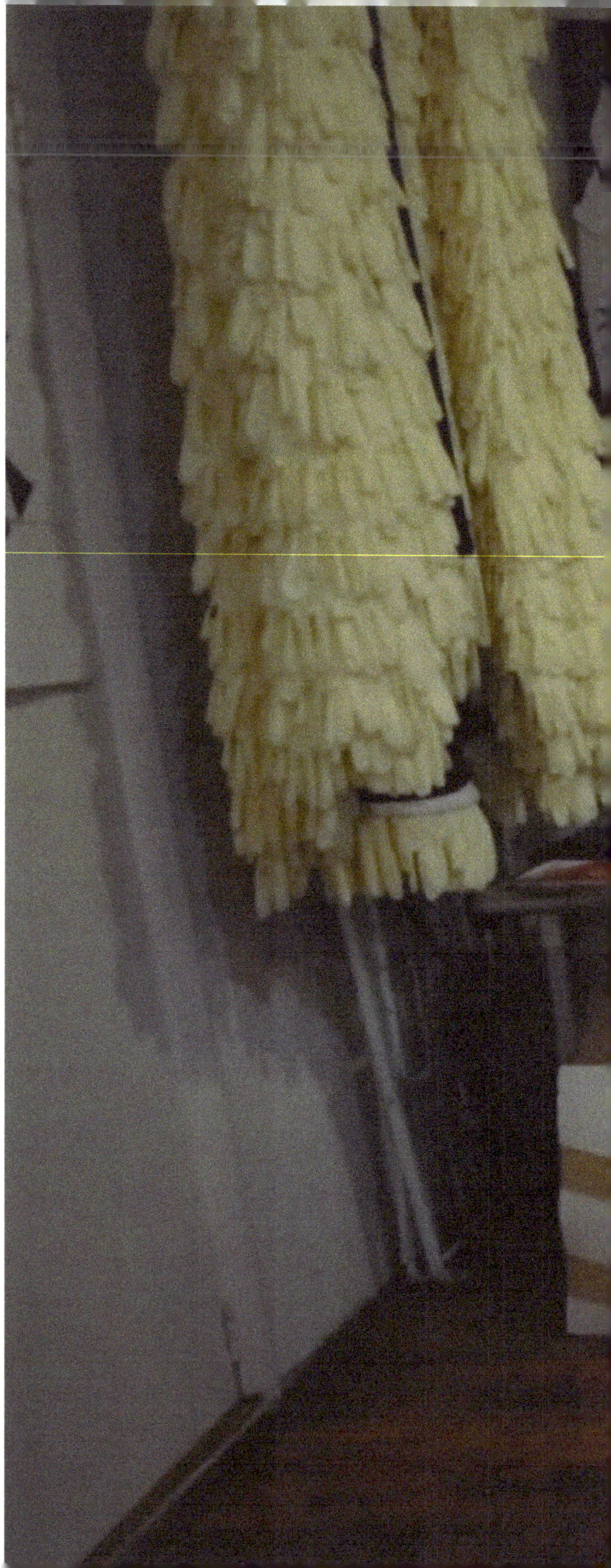

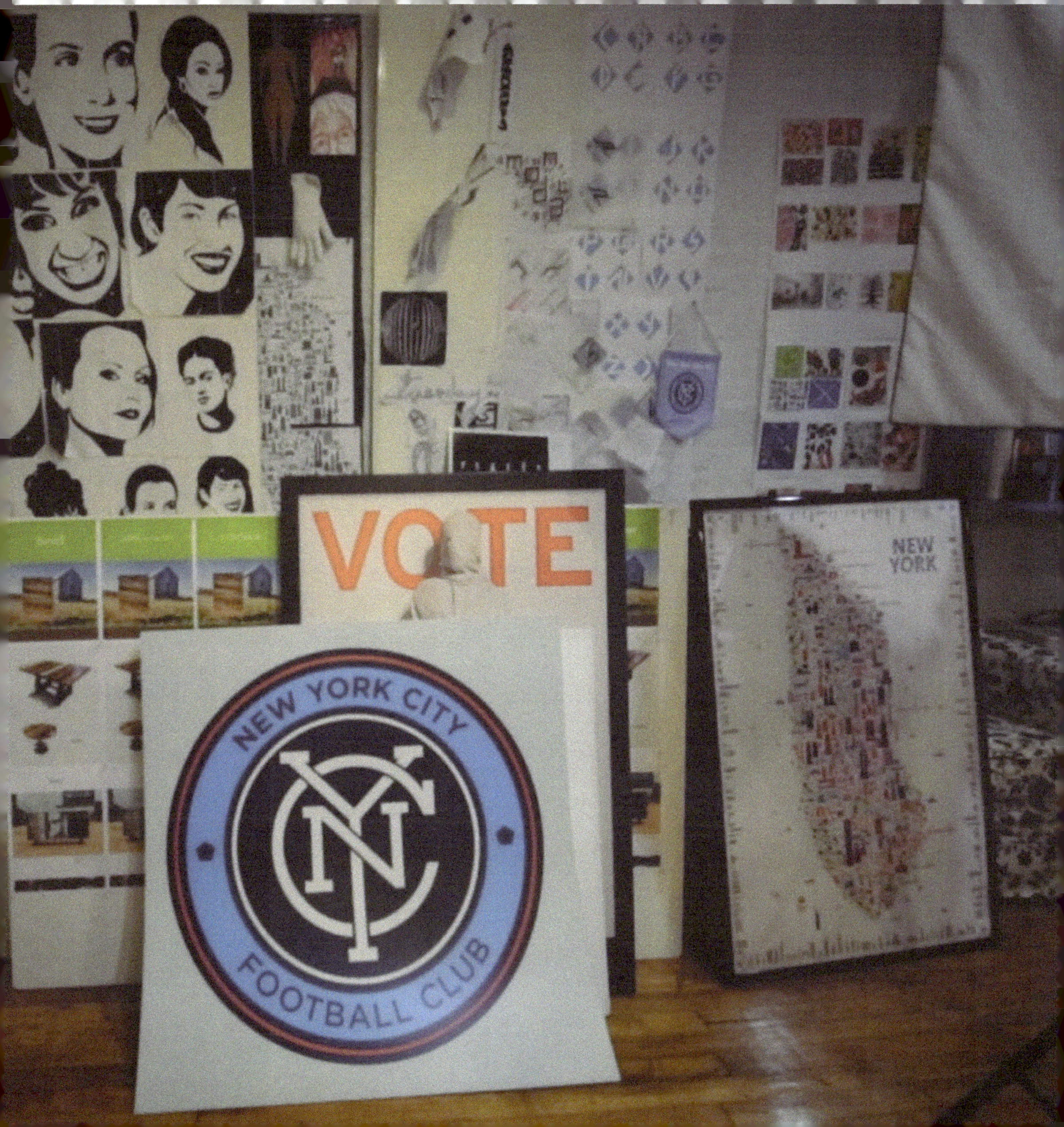

VOTE
NEW YORK CITY
FOOTBALL CLUB
NEW
YORK

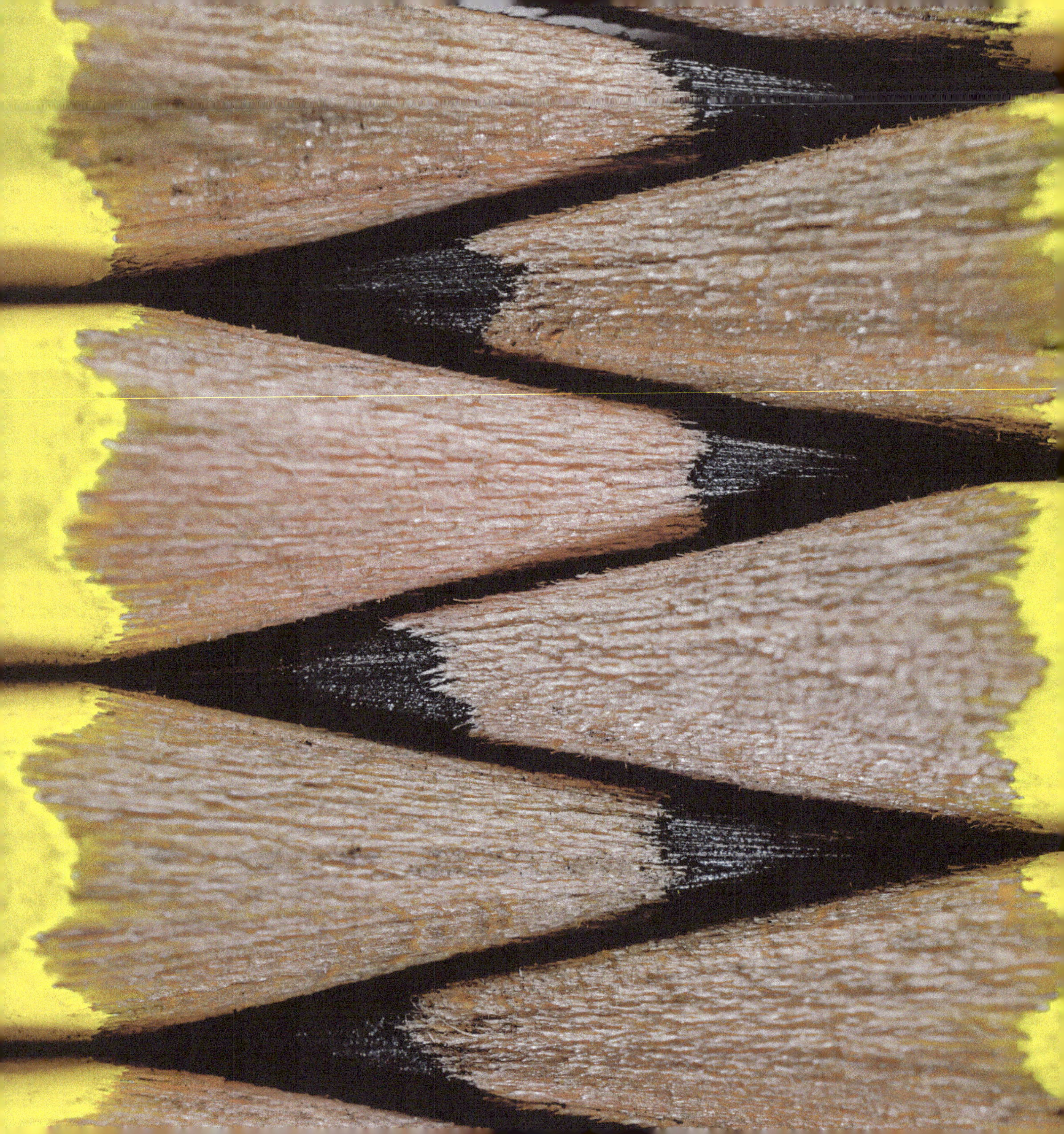

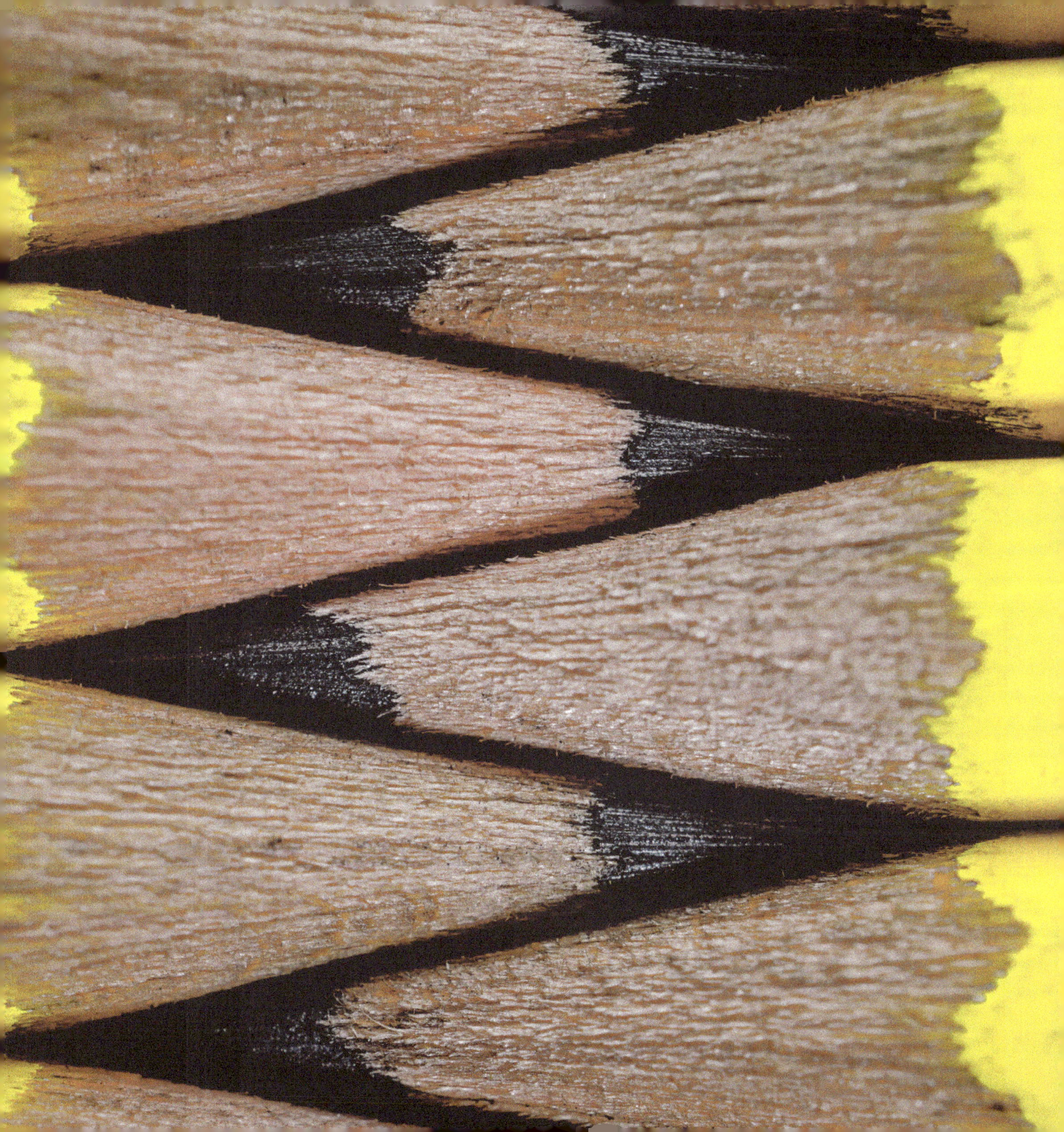

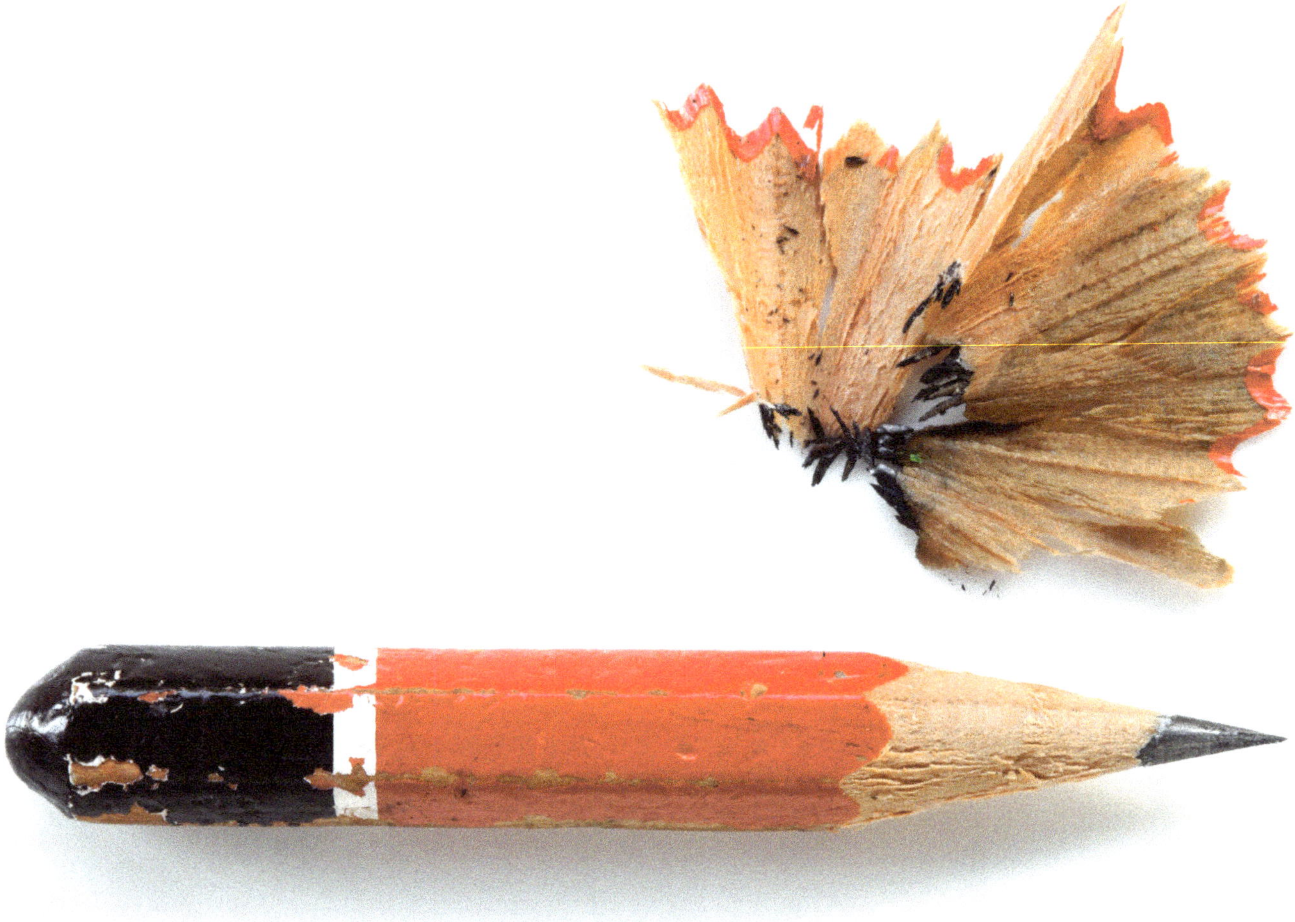

Designing with the Pencil

David Carson, American Graphic Designer and "Godfather of Grunge Design"

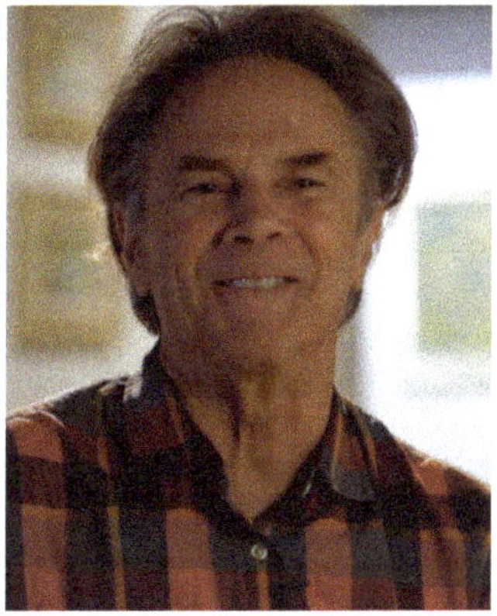

I would say it's hard for me to connect the early memories in some way without a pencil because I was always doodling and always drawing on magazines or making up games with pencils. I can't remember a specific first time, but it seems they've always been with me.

Survival

It's like it's made for your hand. It's a good experience to this day. Even driving today, I realized I was holding a pencil for no particular reason other than it felt good, for lack of a better word, or comfortable. Other things fail if you try to go to that same position. There's just something about a pencil that feels almost like an extension of your hand, or that it just belongs there. I could probably carry one all day. It's just so trouble-free. It's accessible at any time. You don't have to set anything up; it's there. It has a texture, a smell. It has its own experience.

They're just simple, and I'm sure I've never picked one up and not read details that are on there. I don't like new ones, and I don't like long ones. I like them a little bit shorter, and I've been known to use really short ones quite a bit. It's hard to imagine them just disappearing. You've always had people that say, "Oh no, of course it's going to disappear and be replaced." I don't think so. It's held up through some pretty major technology-driven changes, yet there is nothing like a good, solid pencil in your hand, or a beat-up one. It's like a comfort food.

There are other times when you feel like you can't really pick one up and not use it. If I've got one, I'm looking for something I can start doodling on. I may make a few notes or something.

I used to do games as a kid with myself, and later friends, where I would take a pencil and some kind of paper, and I would challenge myself. I would make just some kind of quick little weird shape. I might not even look. Then I would challenge myself to turn that into a face or a person. And I would every time. Never failed.

Then, later, I would do that with friends. I'd say, "Okay, just a weird little shape. I want to turn that into a person, or at least a face," and usually a person with more detail in the face and funny little maybe stick figure body. It was a little game that I did, and a pencil was pivotal to that. I can't imagine doing that with, say, a pen. It might get splotchy or weird.

Early on, it became something to entertain. It was a comfort. I feel those two areas pretty specifically. It was like I could probably hold this all day and not think twice about it. I don't think it's an age thing.

The other thing is I'll look for my pencil, and then finally someone will tell me it's behind my ear.

I was really disappointed because I found a really cool one the other day that was round, no paint, really well done, and I was like, "This is the coolest pencil ever," so I stole it from the hotel where I was staying. and I was just like, "I'm going to fly all the way back from Peru with this pencil. It's so cool." Then I realized, when I was driving to the airport and went to put it behind my ear, like I normally would, that I had my sunglasses on, so it really wasn't working. I was kind of frustrated with that, because it was really bright, and I didn't really want to give up the sunglasses. I finally compromised, and I would never do this normally, but under these circumstances, I really wanted this pencil for the trip, so I put it in my top pocket. It was a sharp one, and I was a little worried about maybe poking through my shirt, so I put it with the lead up. Then I thought, That might not be a really good position for the lead. That's how it stayed most of the trip, and I got it from Peru to where I am now in Florida.

I'm really bummed I didn't bring it today, because it's really special. For me, I don't know that I appreciated them as much when I was younger, but to find a round, smooth one that appears to be real wood with little varnish, or hopefully nothing on it, that's a real find, and those feel good.

You have to start drawing when it enters your hand.

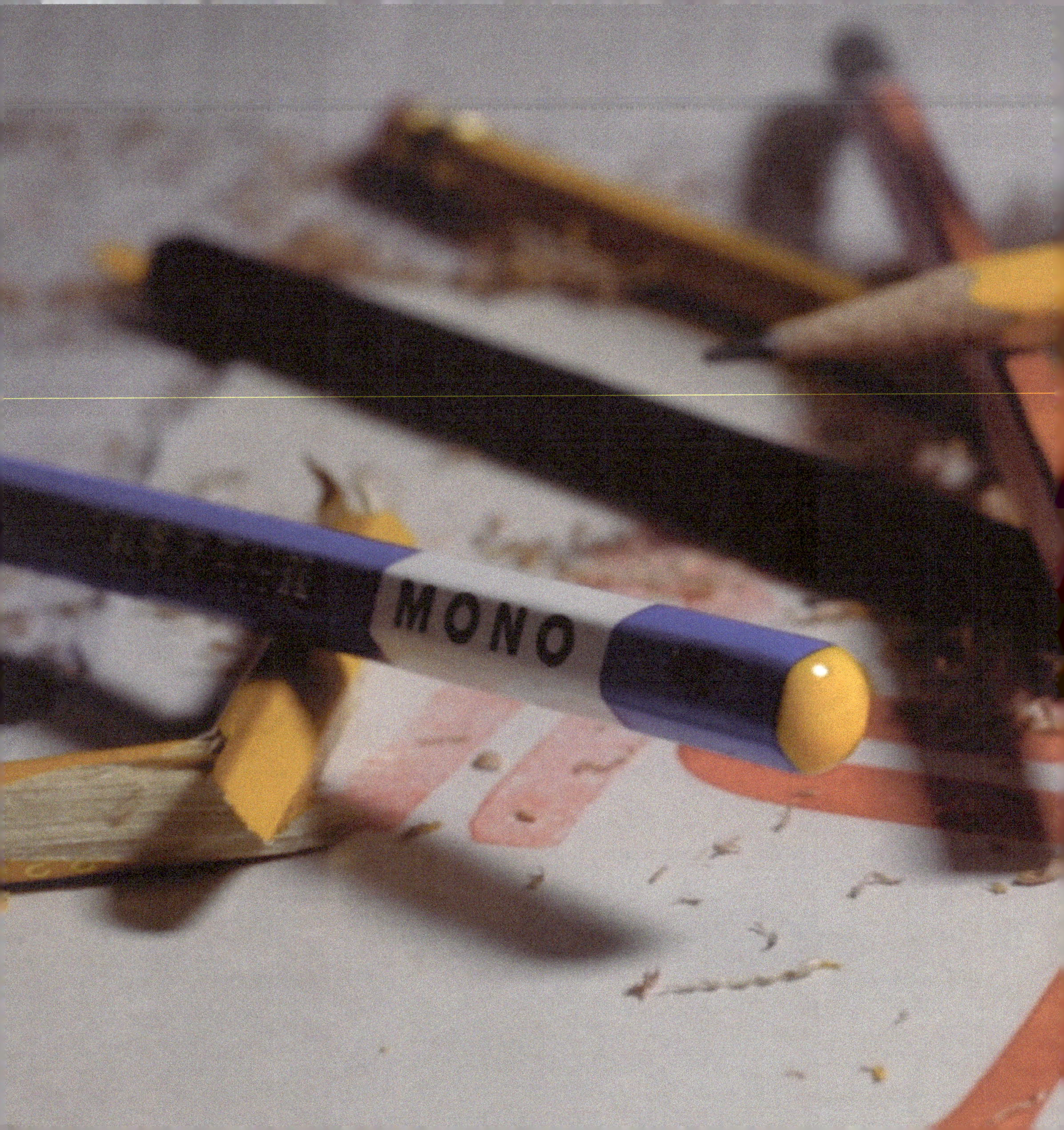
MONO

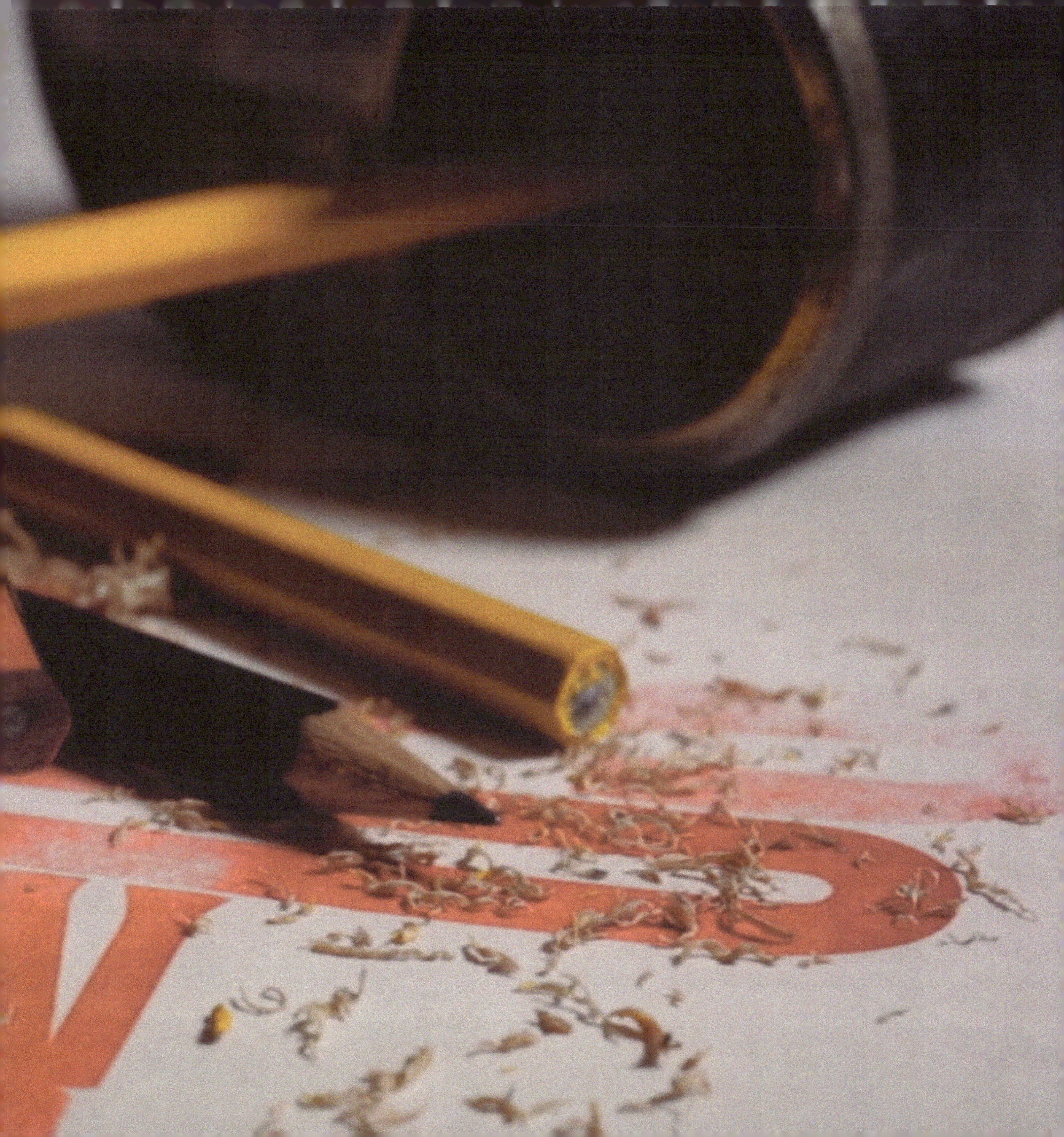

It's almost as though it is electric or it is hooked up to something because, when it goes in the hand, something needs to start being done, and I don't always feel that with other devices.

Throw out the Old to Pursue the New

I don't think there's ever a point where you make that decision, and say, "Okay, pencils are over. Gone. Let's get rid of these boxes, or whatever." They find their place, they find new uses, and they find their life changes a bit.

I worked on a book called "The End of Print." It's in its fifth printing now. Did print go away? No, it hasn't died. It's role changed dramatically and will continue to, much like vinyl records, but I don't think anybody would get rid of vinyl records; quite the opposite actually. No, there's a place for it. There's a place for new technologies and the older, tried ones. No, there's no reason to get rid of them.

I know a lot of teachers still use pencils. They are important in design schools, to do a sketch by pencil.

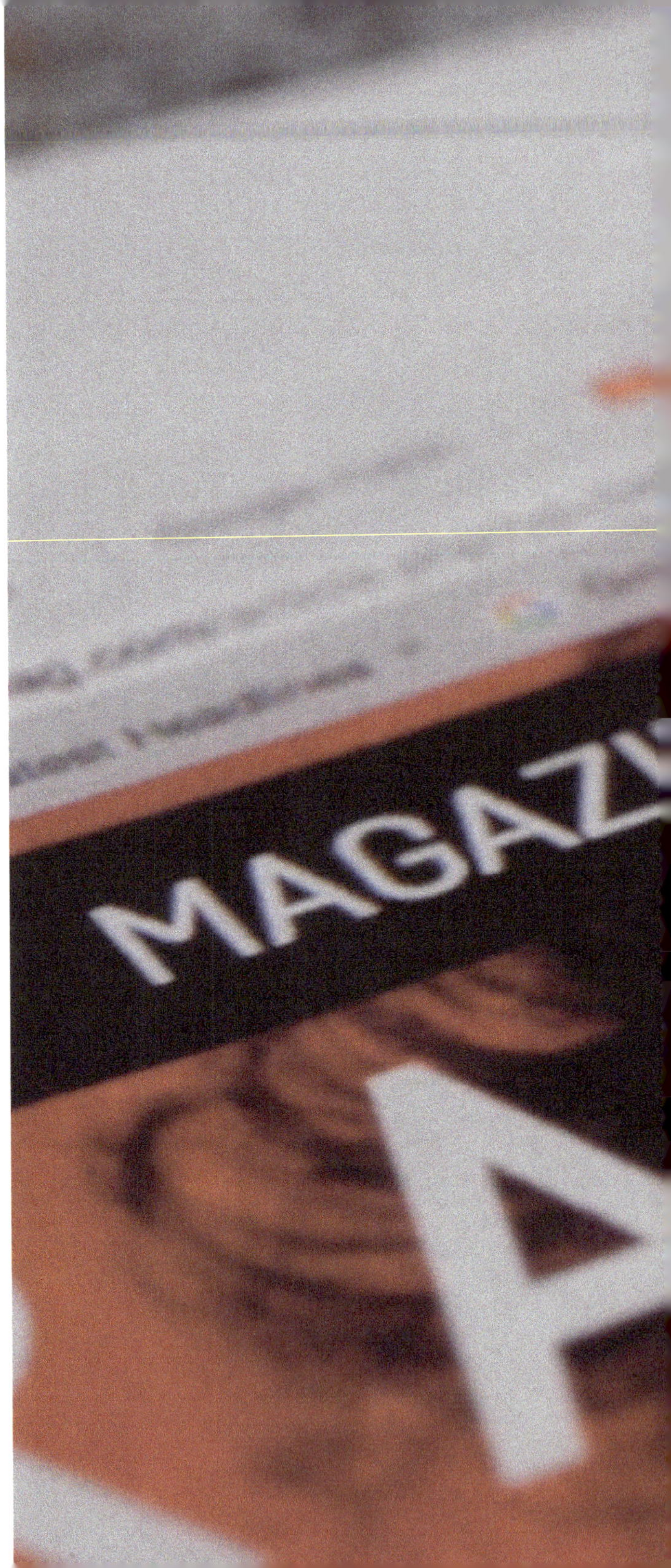

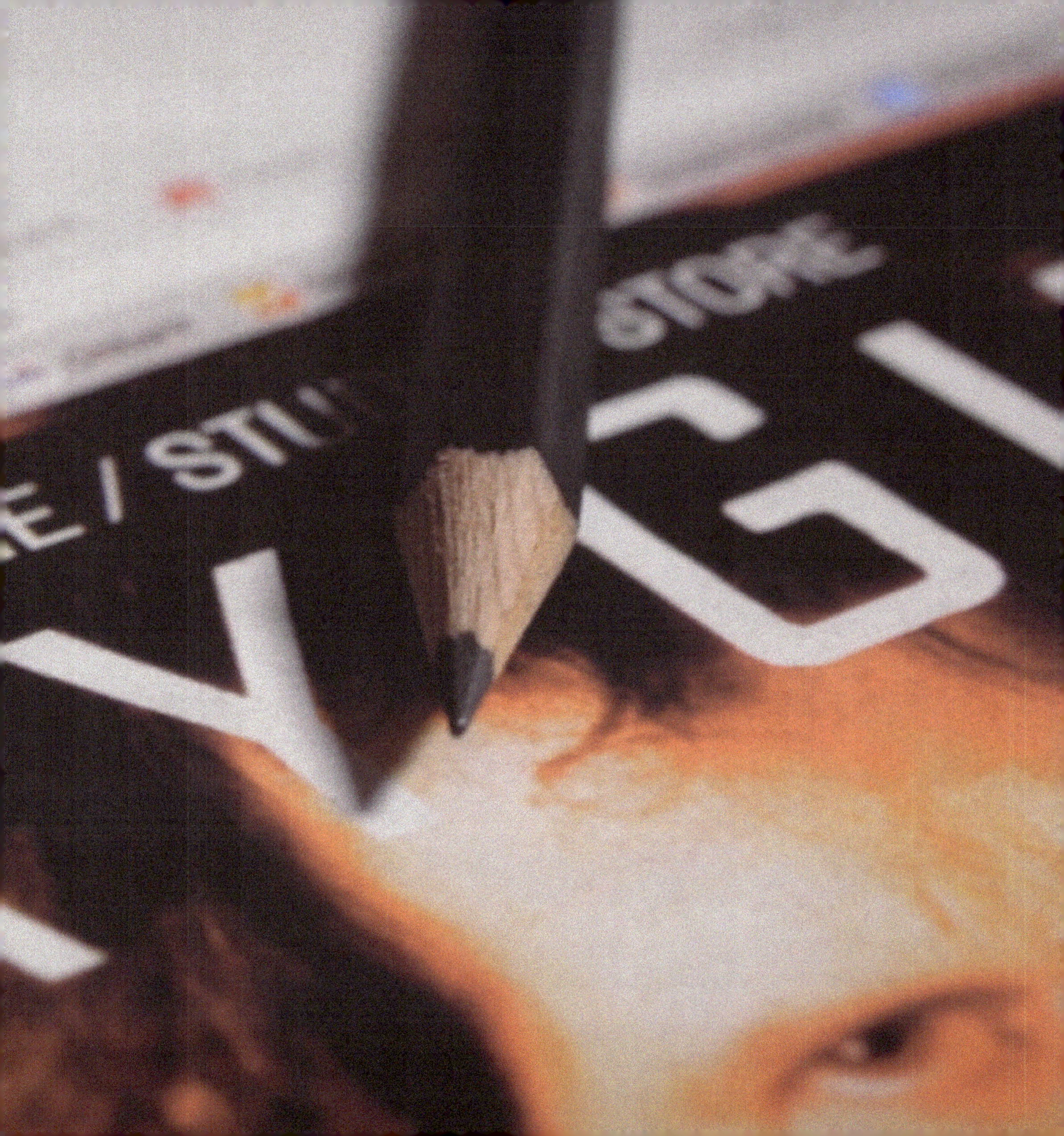

Some of the best logos, advertising, design work, your branding work, I guarantee started with a pencil, even to this day. I don't mean a new electronic pencil or a stylus; I mean a wood pencil. That's going on as we speak. They may more quickly go to other technology, but the starting point is still largely the pencil. There's no good reason to stop that basic ideation. Some will, and I say, "Fine. If that works for you to not make a sketch first in pencil, if you want to go to the computer, if that works for you, that's fine." I'm ultimately more interested in the final result, but if it works for someone like it often does for me, and many people I know, just try a few ideas first by pencil. And when you're happy with something, then go to the computer. By all means, keep doing that. It's hard for me to imagine pencils disappearing.

Just recently, I was attempting to sell some prints of my earlier work, and something struck me. To give them added value, I was asked, and of course agreed, to sign them, but only in pencil. Some are one-offs, some are limited print editions, so they're pretty rare, and we're hoping the value is substantial. That's all relative, of course. To make sure they had the added value, it was imperative that they be signed in pencil, not pen.

A person I'm working with who knows more about prints and selling originals and all that arrived with—I wish I knew how many and which ones—only pencils. I thought, There's something really interesting there. It's value is absolutely perceived as greater if it's signed in pencil than pen, and of course no comparison with any kind of stamp or mark like that. That's pretty lasting power. I don't think that's going anywhere soon.

Since I had that experience, I realize whenever I see signed art now, it's in pencil, the expensive ones. That's one of its greatest testaments. If you want to add extra value to this original piece of art, be sure you are using a pencil. Do not use a pen, much less a marker.

Starting Point

In my work now, I'd say the starting point is pretty

much always the pencil, but it may be before I even think. It's maybe in the first meeting with the client, or a perspective client, or even on the phone. I'm probably writing down in pencil a few things I'm thinking of, some ideas, and I'm probably sketching, too. We're talking about the overall brief. I'm already trying little things and making little mental notes. "Okay, that could work. I could do … Yeah, uh-huh …" And get back to them.

Early, before the even actual design process, and then later when I'm going through the early briefing and some of the instructional phase, back in the studio or whatever, the first thing I'm going to do is rough out some ideas in pencil, to different degrees.

Sometimes you know sooner where you need to go, so you get on the computer. But, initially, what better way to start? I don't want a pen that leaks, and even if it doesn't leak, it's just not the same. It feels cheaper to me than a pencil. It's a starting point and different degrees.

I have sheets of notes from meetings, and when I get done, especially if they've given me an agenda of things to do, an outline, I just have a page full of doodling by pencil, and it's great. Maybe some keywords, maybe not. Probably a lot of pictures of waves and surfing. A lot of surfboards. I was forever drawing surfboards. I always had trouble getting the symmetric right. I could get one rail really good, and then the other one, never. I always had trouble getting this together.

It's just like an old friend. You don't have to figure it out. How does it open, what color am I going to get? There's none of that.

Memory

The pencil could be the first memory stick because, when I was little, I was always having to write thank-you notes, or any holiday notes, to my grandparents. They were always done in pencil, and I hand-wrote the envelope. I always tried to do the best cursive writing I could. As a result, more years than I want to admit later, I remember the address where my grandparents

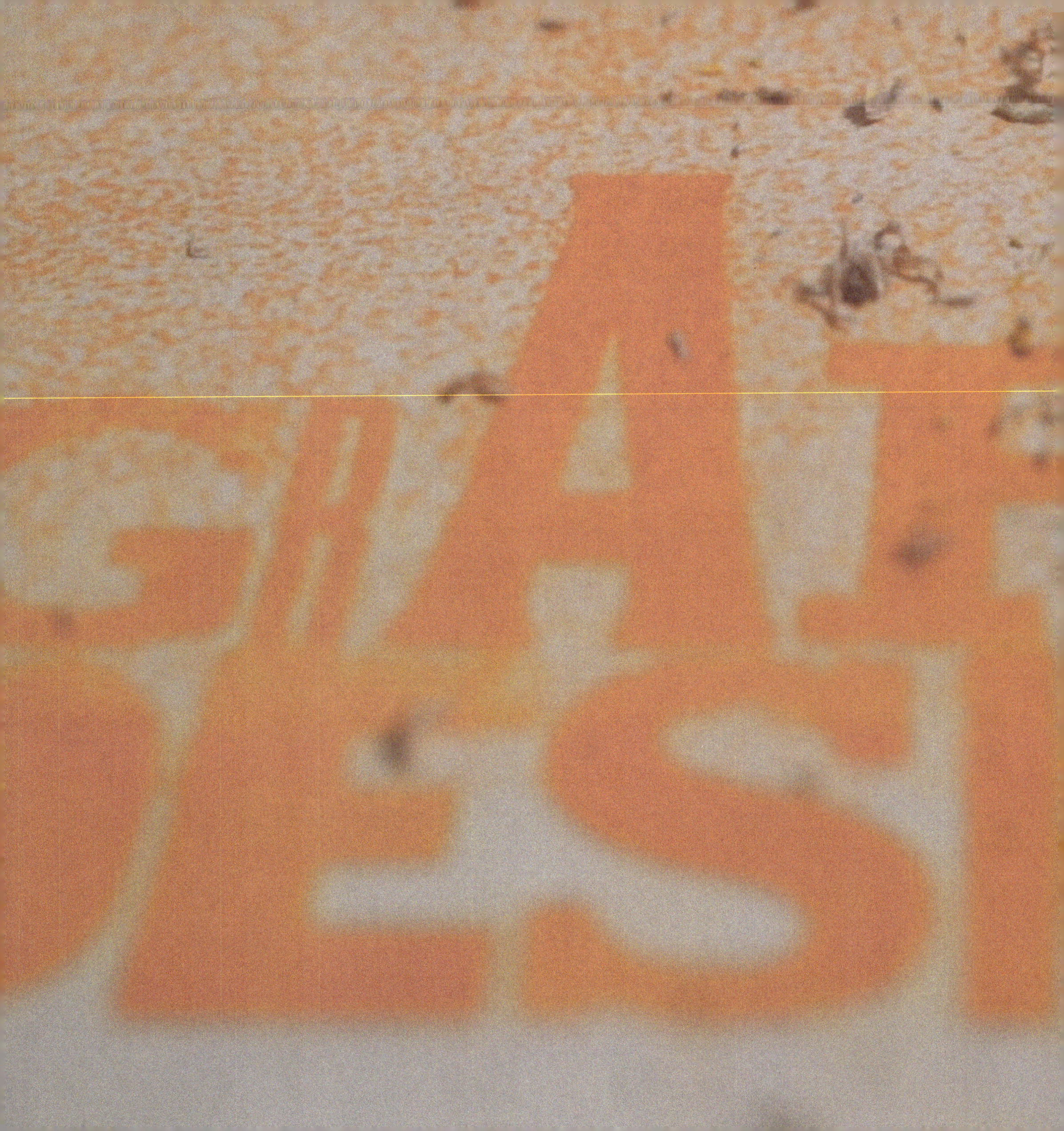

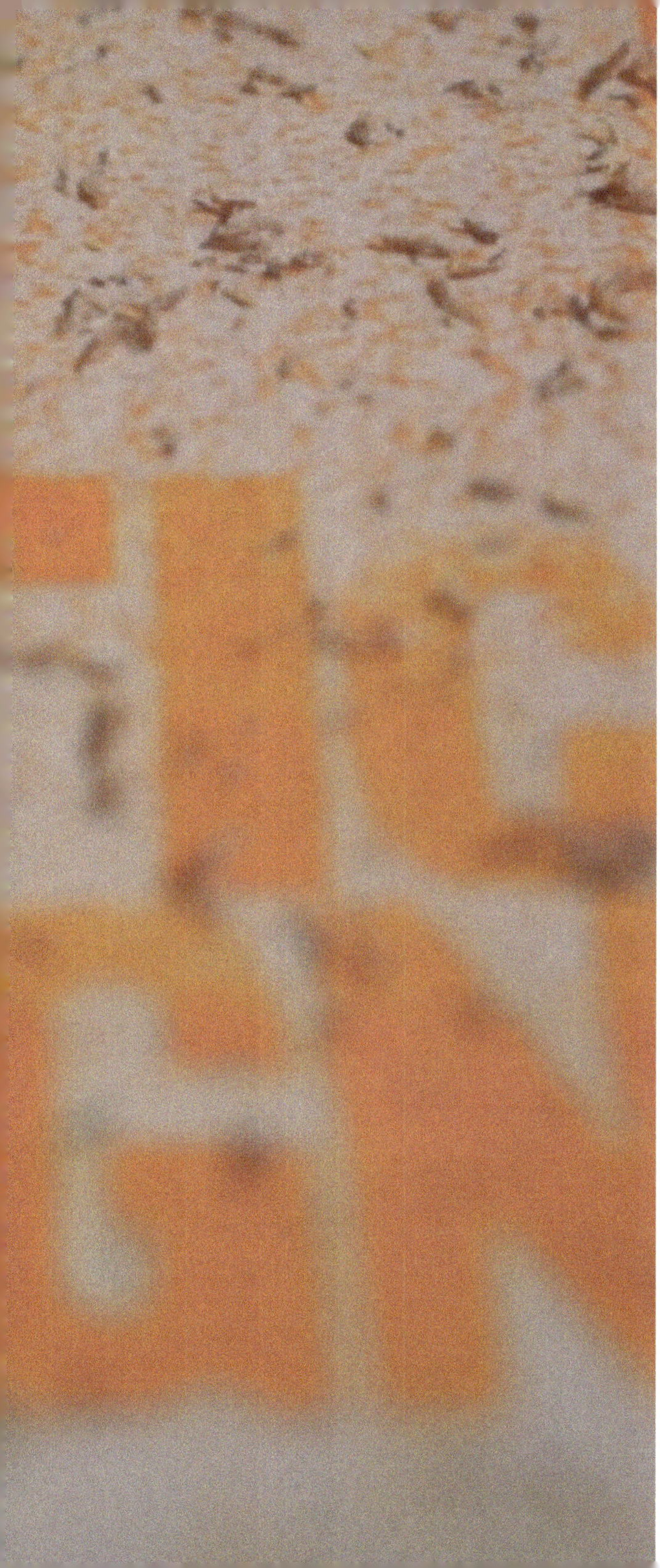

lived. Some of that had to be from me trying to make a really nice "five." I can see it now, to be sure the capital "P" looked like a capital and you could still read it. Don't forget that little dent in the "R."

Just like that, decades later, I've remembered the name. The same thing doesn't happen on a computer, at least for me, because if I wanted to write a letter to my grandparents, and I wish I still could, I'd just hit a button, and their address would come up. I might not even see it. It would just be on there, sent to them.

I would have to really work at memorizing this thing that, before now, is ingrained in another sense. Not just visual but physical. And thinking it through, I don't want that "O" to look like a "A" or vice versa. I'm sure that has some effect on things I remember. I'm not a big one to say it's bad or it's worse, that it's changed, but it has changed.

I have all sorts of family and people I write to pretty regular that I couldn't tell you their email. I had to fill one in this morning, and I thought, "I have no idea what it is. I just hit that button, and now it's not coming up." It's a memory stick. It just is. It's just kind of a feel good thing. I wouldn't go so far as to say it's a security blanket or something like that, but it's comfortable and feels good, and something good is probably going to happen if I've got one in my hand.

Change

There seems to have been various attempts, especially since computers came in, to replicate pencils. I'd say, for me personally, they're all failures. I still don't use a mechanical pencil, but many do, for several reasons. Maybe they don't have the background or heritage that I do with pencils. I don't know how that's working out with younger school kids and stuff, what they're given. I'm pretty sure they're not being given a stylus yet, although I could be wrong on that, too. It's a great homage to the pencil that these latest technologies are still the newest one, yet they're calling it a pencil. That's putting the original pencil on a bit of a shrine or an altar. We're respecting this thing so much. Then, this day, all the money, research, and testing that we've put into these new technologies, and we're still calling it a pencil. You hold it just like you would a real pencil. A real pencil. That's a whole other topic or phrase.

To me, it's like, "No. That's never going to feel like a real pencil to me, but at least I've been trained to hold it in that way so maybe I can figure out a way to work it." Even with that, there's always going to be both.

I have the pencil from the hotel that I've been writing myself little notes and stuff with. I could have tried to type something in or whatever, but no. It just works.

I was actually a little offended when they called this newest stylus a pencil. It's like, "Come on. Come on." If that becomes the new pencil to a new generation, I still can't think the other ones are going to disappear completely. There's probably a place for both, and I'm kind of curious to try some of the newer ones and more technology-driven ones. That will still come from the love of the original and that they still feel good. It will always be the fall back. Then, when I have to write notes to myself, and I'm bored to death in a meeting, drawing waves and surfboards, a pencil for sure. The real pencil, I should say.

I have to think that the original pencil, like the one I'm holding, the one I meant to bring that didn't have any paint and was not beveled—it was round—those aren't going anywhere or aren't changing much. I suspect the technical ones may try to feel more like the originals. I haven't actually seen or held the newest version, but my guess is the goal is to make you think it really is a pencil. A real pencil.

Who knows on the technology end? It may be something completely different. By then, maybe your eyes just move, and it draws for you. I don't know. But I think the basic pencil is pretty hard to improve on. I don't see anything replacing it. I can see things being used with it in different areas or different things.

A pen feels good in your pocket, and a pencil feels good in your hand. That's a big difference. Your pants pocket for the pen. It feels a little nerdy up here [in your shirt], but yeah, a pen works in my pocket, but a pencil works in my hand.

Future

In terms of negative aspects, for me, I never liked the erasing part of it. The residue it leaves, it never seems to completely erase it well. The erasers were always a bit of a trouble spot. Maybe less harmful to have in your mouth. Certainly the metal. I've ground down a lot of those. I have this vivid image of a short little pencil, no more eraser, and a lot of teeth marks.

Even a better memory probably would be in junior high school, in the lunchroom. This had been quite a while now, but of course that's all you used—pencils. At lunch, we used to take them and throw them up. They would stick in the ceiling all over the cafeteria. The teachers would get really mad, and the lunch ladies would go nuts. Then some poor janitor was always taking these things down. It was pretty fun.

Years later, it would be shoes hung over wires, doing the same thing. I don't know if this was early tagging or not. You had to be sure no one was looking.

The thing I do remember with pencils is you never really erase. There's still always something there, whether it's even the indention, and then you've got all this eraser dust falling on your lap or still on the paper.

Somebody just handed me a more mechanical pencil, and the thing that first struck me is how cold it is. I have this warm, friendly instrument here that I can draw a wave, and a family member, and write somebody's name that I'm in love with or whatever, and this thing is cold. So, immediately, it's standoffish. I may warm up to it, and it may warm up, but that's what struck me when it was handed to me. "Wow, it's really cold," where the wood-cased pencil just feels like part of my hand. That was my first reaction.

I never liked the shape of the flat, wide pencil. There are probably people who love them for different things. Not me. No. Pencils should be round, but of course, I'm used to the beveled ones. The principles are the same.

Maybe if you grew up, and it's all you have, you're going to get used to it, and maybe a stylus does become a pencil for you, but it's going to be pretty fun when you then discover the real pencil.

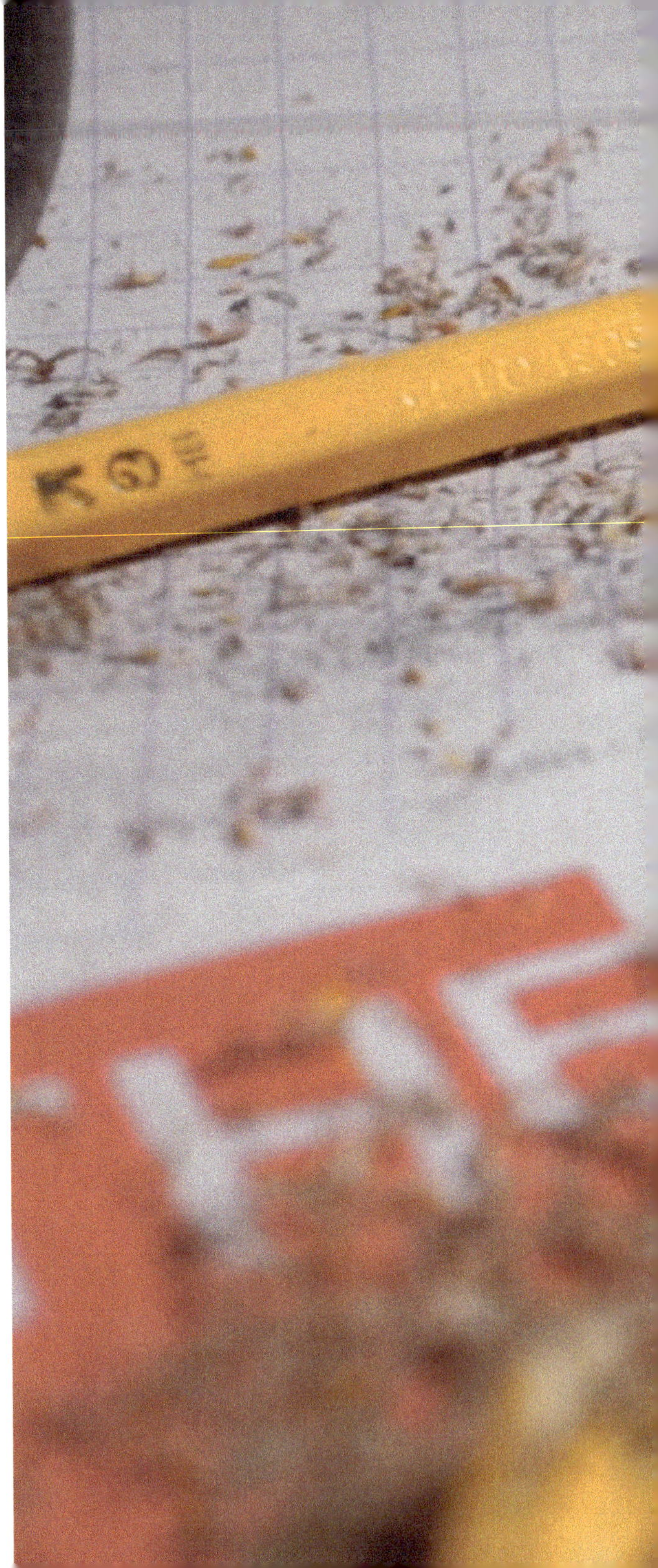

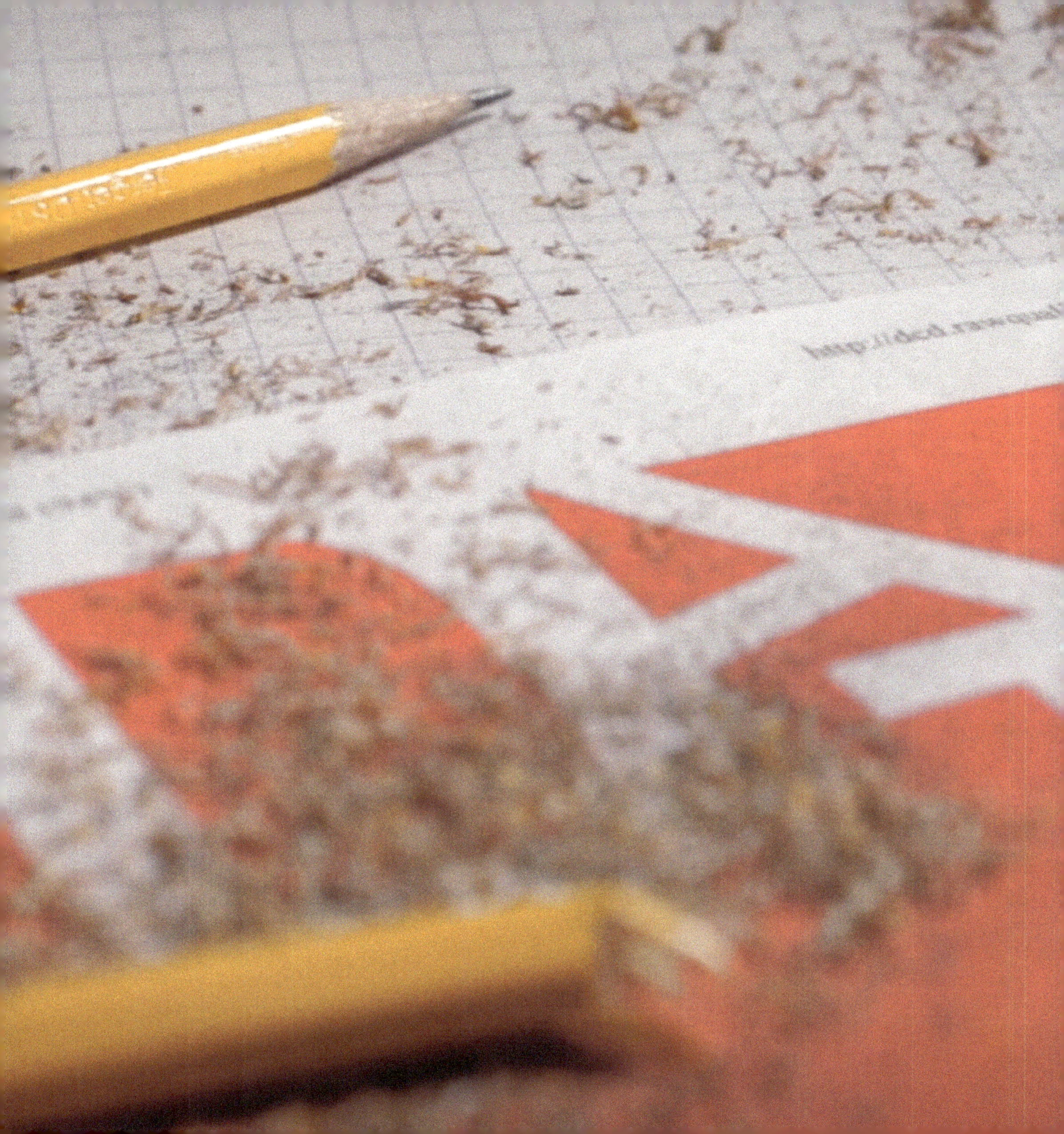

Ideas

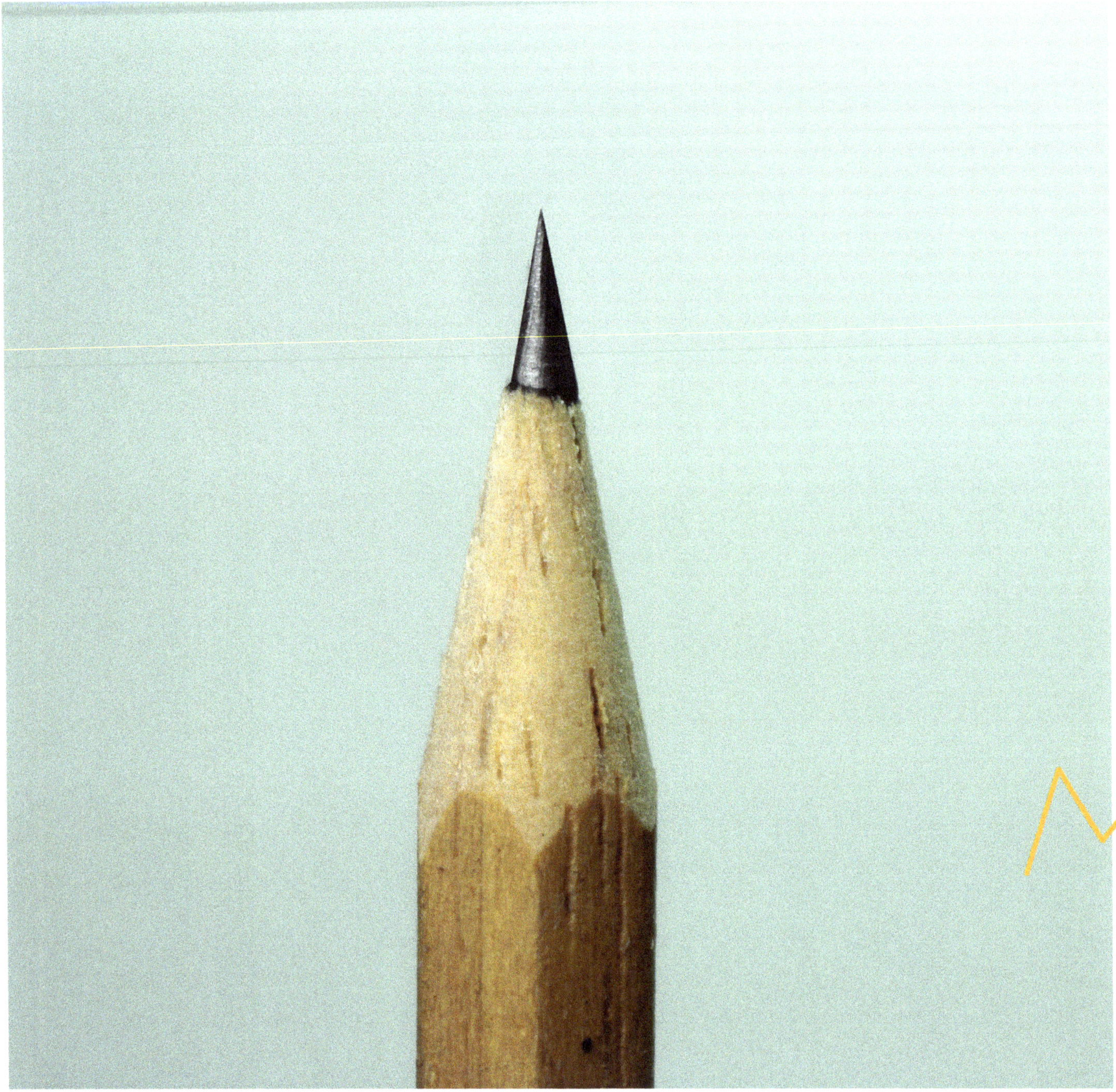

Found It's Place

Michael Wesch, Professor of Digital Anthropology

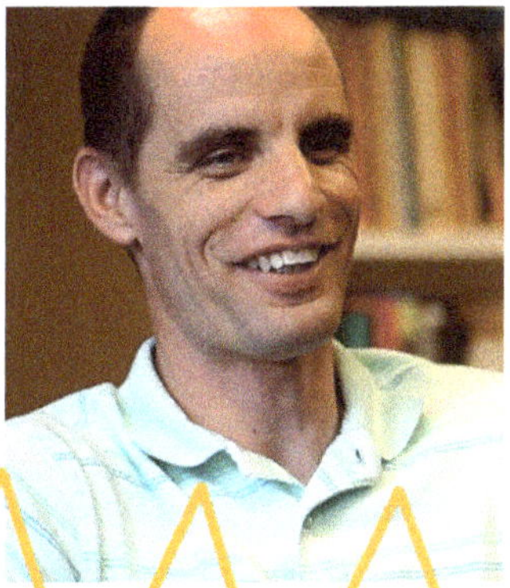

I don't think the pencil's really worried about dying. I think it's kind of found its place, and it's going to live there for a while. But it's been through some rough times. I mean, imagine, like say the witch trials, and you're the pencil. Somebody's using you to write down names of witches and stuff. I'd be sick of that, too. Let somebody else do that.

Working Out Who You Are

The pencil was on the rise through the 1800s, and then you also had a rise in literacy. The other thing going on at the same time is a rise in everything we think we know about individualism and how we think about ourselves. Who we are as a self was being worked out at this time. Think about how important defining who you are and shaping who you are is, and

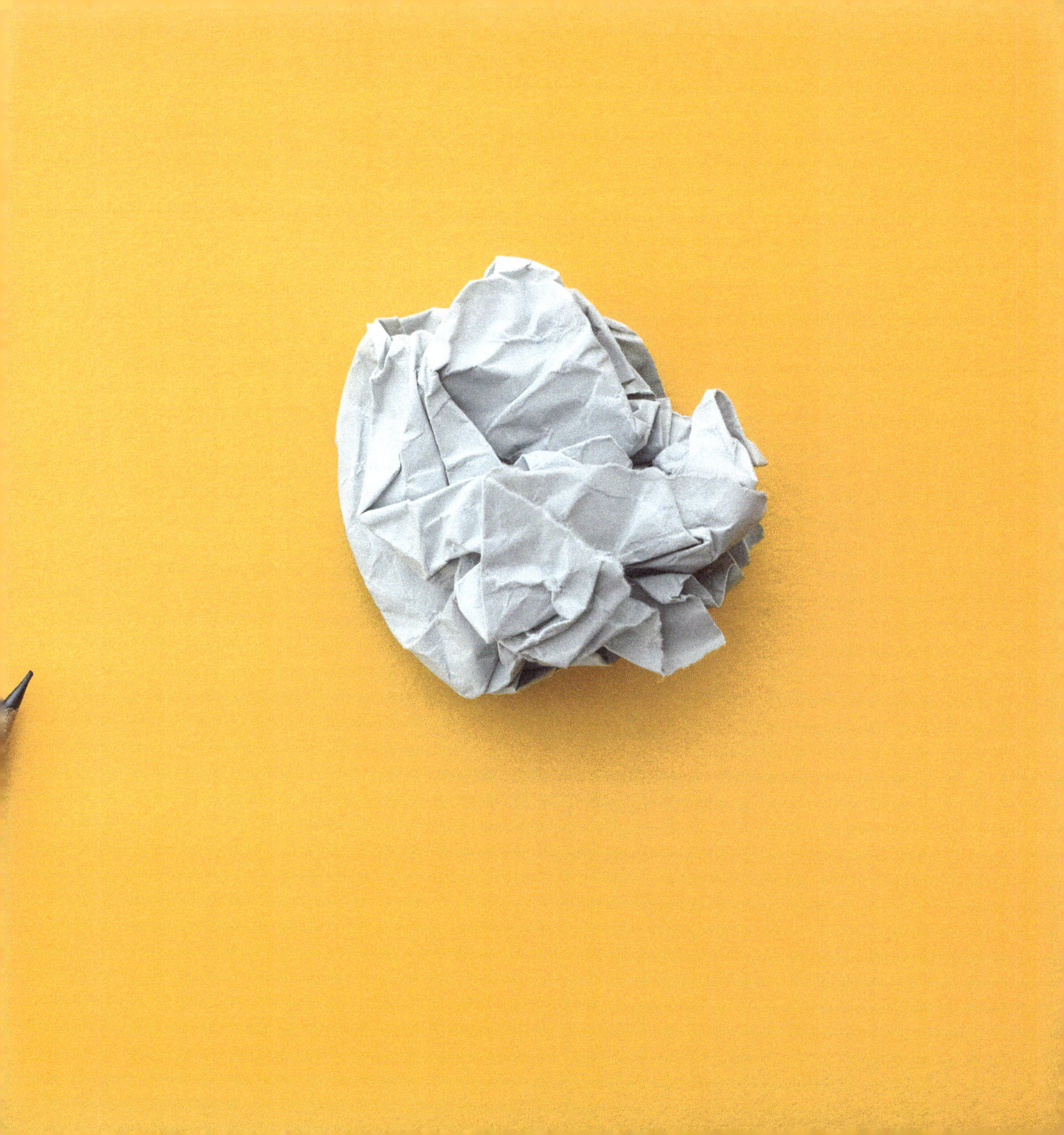

suddenly, most people have the capacity to write stuff down and reflect on it. That's definitely going to have some effect on how we think about ourselves. The ability to sketch out a thought and work with it. Just the idea that you can move something internal out into the external world. And now it's this thing you can manipulate. You might come back to it five or ten years later, and it looks different. That's definitely going to shape quite profoundly, the way we think about ourselves.

Philosophers suggest this is the time when we start trying to figure out who we really are. I know that sounds strange to say, but prior to this, most people didn't worry about the question: "Who am I really?" For most of human history, you were just going to do what your parents did. And who you were was shaped by your relationships. You kind of defined yourself by your relationships. Suddenly, you're in this space where you're really trying to create yourself. That's new. Writing, literacy, the pencil—that's all wrapped up with this whole project of trying to create yourself.

You can actually say it's the core project of our lives now. It dominates our whole life. "Who am I?" And the pencil is wrapped up with that. We all have moments where the pencil is pretty key to that development. You're actually kind of working out who you are as you're writing and thinking, and all that becomes wrapped up as part of this same process. It definitely has shaped how it happens.

Memorization

Think of something as simple as whether or not you can remember phone numbers from twenty years ago. Now, your phone holds all the cell phone numbers, so you don't remember them. Or you think about Google; there's this question from Nick Carr that famously asks, "Is Google making us dumb?"

Pencils are similar in that regard. It's a pretty serious thing to start writing. A lot of our mental capacities have been diminished since the advent of writing. If you look at The Iliad and The Odyssey, they were oral tales. But can you imagine people apparently memorizing the equivalent of six to eight hundred pages of text? And there are still pockets of cultures in the world today that do that. And so we know it happens.

That's a different capacity than what we have today. For example, so few students today can have any lines of poetry memorized which used to be a common thing. I think it is sort of special to be able to encounter life with some of that, to have a poem memorized that you can call forth at some difficult moment or a trying time. There's something lost there. Every technology takes a little away, but it also gives us something.

Digital Writing

When you move into digital text, you're moving into a space where the possibilities aren't completely explored yet. So, where we're at now with digital text is so mystifying. It's like, here you have this text that's appearing before you on the screen, but behind that text, even for a single letter, would be a string of ones and zeros that would be incomprehensible to you. Because you'd have the font style, and you'd have the letter itself, and then, these days, it would be adapting to the screen resolution. There's so much going on there to make that thing appear as it does.

And so, if you just take one of those things, like the separation of form and content when you write with a pencil, it just is what it is. It's this thing, and the style of it, the font, the everything. There is the physicality of it. But, with digital, you're just unhinging all of that, and you're minimally assigning form, like how it looks. It can be encoded by one document. That's a huge list of stuff, whether it's a CSS document or whatever it might be.

You can have this huge document that's just defining what that thing's going to look like. And then you have this letter itself as the content. So, you have the content and the form. Once you separate those two things, that creates immense possibilities. But now you could take it another step and say, "Well, not only are we going to have form and content separate, so this thing can look different in different spaces." This also allows people, who have no idea how to make something look pretty, still provide content. Then other people can make it look pretty, or they can grab a theme and make it look pretty.

But now you can also, in the creation of the text itself, say, "You know what? I don't want to write alone. Why don't all of you come in here and help me write this? And now I'm going to invite millions of people in to work on my document," which you can actually do. So, now the production of the document is collaborative in a way that we've never really collaborated.

Media really does shape what can be said, how it can be said, who can say it, who can hear it, how messages will be stored, if they will be stored, and who will access that stored information. All of that stuff is shaped by a medium.

You start thinking about what a medium is, if it's not a tool? I think if we go to the word itself, a medium stands between you and I, and it shapes our conversation. I often think of media as the ultimately shaping of relationships. They mediate relationships, therefore mediating our conversations. You can actually say that our culture is nothing but a collection of conversations that are constantly going.

Now, if you suddenly throw media in there, that shapes those conversations in different ways. It shapes what's being said, how it's being said, and so on. Suddenly, you have a different culture. And that is going to operate at all levels.

If you look at our economy, our economics have been completely transformed by digital technology already. For example, looking at Wall Street, 80% of trades are done by algorithms. Humans can't even keep up with this stuff. News comes out about something happening over at Apple or IBM, then that stock will bump up, down, wherever it might go. But that bump is about four seconds long. So, we don't even have time to read the headline before the computers have already made the adjustment. That's all happening in that space.

Then, of course, you have the advertising space. Think about our whole market and how there's sort of this database of the mundane about our lives that's being shaped out of all that. But you could go through all levels of society—from the economy, to our social organization, to our family structure, to our religious beliefs—and you will find ways in which shifts in technology are shaping each one of those domains. And the pencil had a part in that.

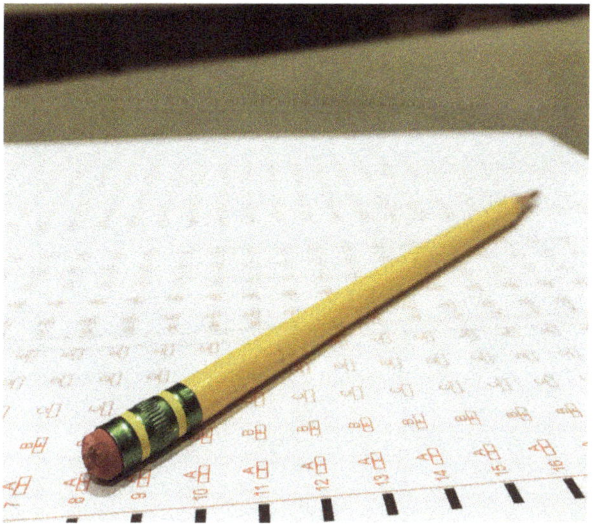

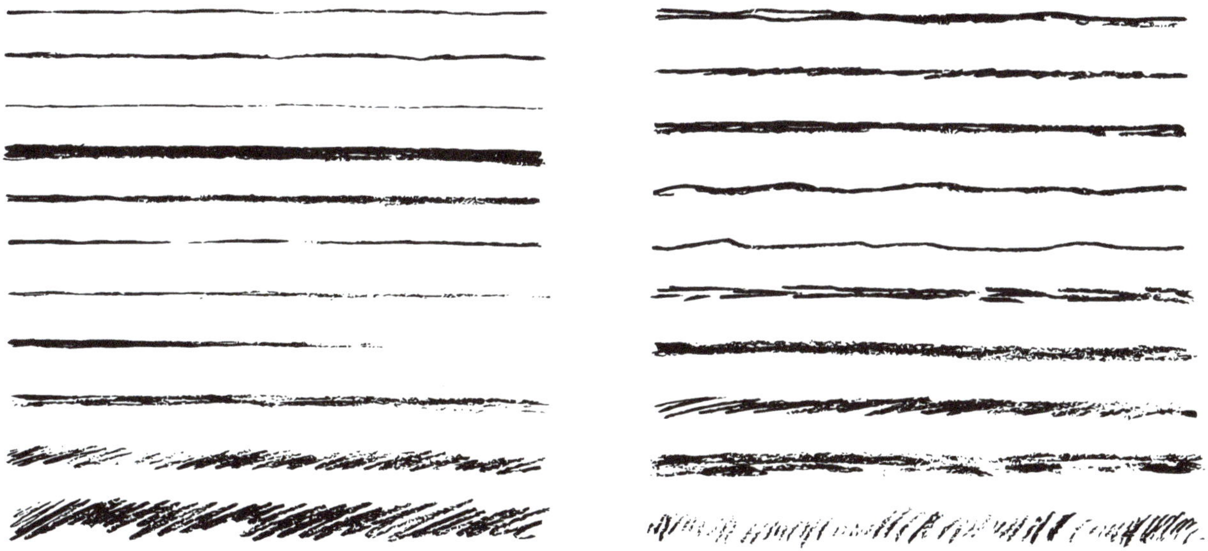

Externalization

Laura Busche

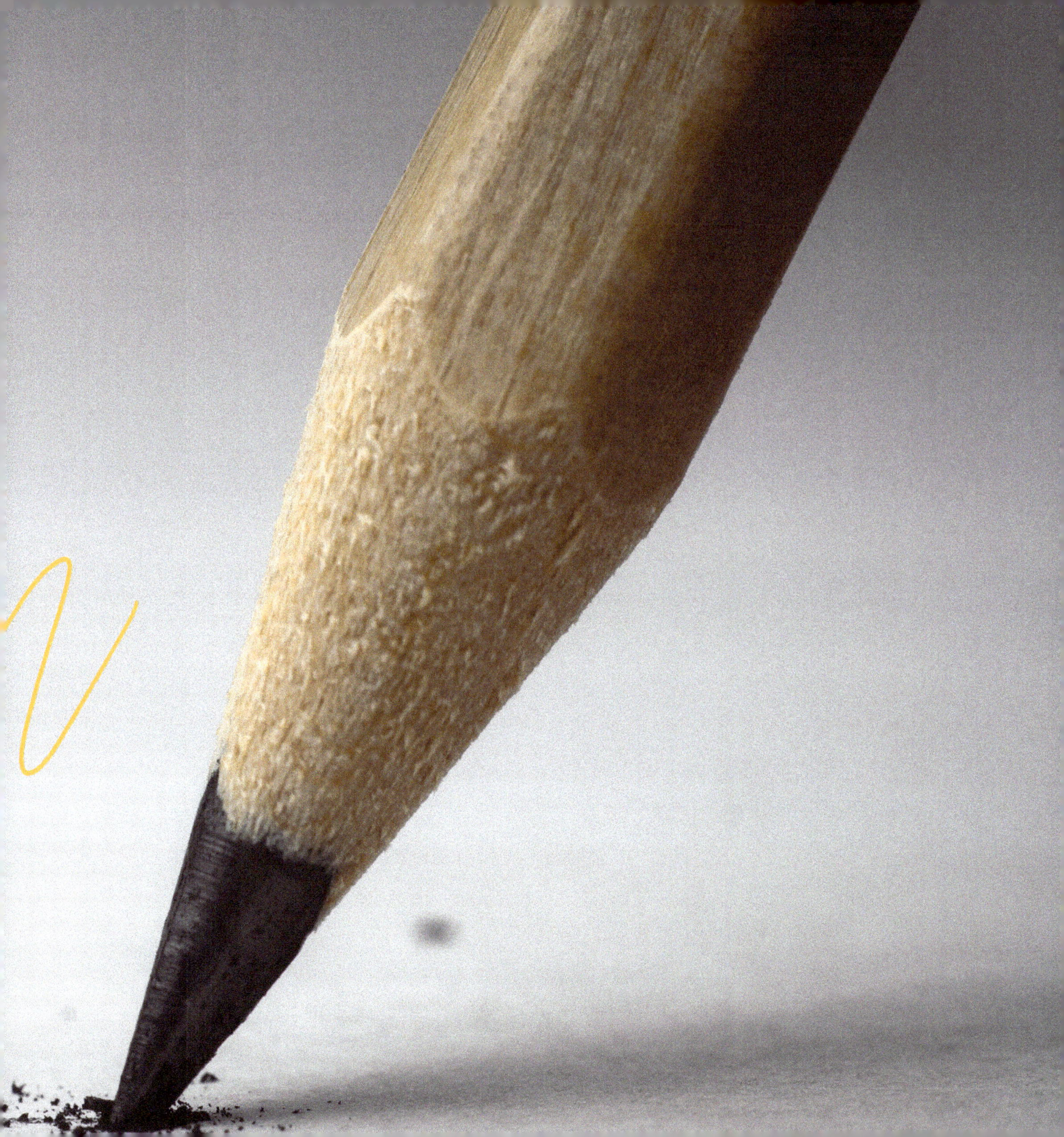

The pencil serves our brain because it is a tool we use to externalize our ideas. We have a short-term memory, we have a long-term memory, and we have an external memory. Sometimes, even more so in this saturated world of ours, the two first memories start falling short because we are just using up our capacities. So, the external memory, our third kind of memory, the pencil suits this, because it allows us to externalize our thoughts.

Both screens and paper give us unique outlets to externalize our thoughts. That is clear. The difference is which one we learn to use first and that feels more comfortable to us. Basically, which one feels like our own skin? For children today, that'll be different than from previous generations who probably learned how to design, sketch, and write on paper. The interesting challenge here is to find whatever works best for you, and whatever allows you to concentrate more.

Now, there are some experiments and tests that have been performed in this sense, and what they conclude is that, if a person is using technology—if the person is using a tablet—somehow they do not know how to use the software package behind it. That creates a learning curve. And that creates stress. If you are good at using these kinds of gadgets and devices, then it'll feel natural to you. But if you're not, you will feel the extra effort. That is going to frustrate some of the ideas that might eventually come out of the ideation process.

There's this freedom that comes with paper and pencil that you don't get from other kinds of externalization. When you're in front of a piece of paper, and you're writing with a pencil, your strokes are rough. They're still incomplete. They're still indeterminate. When that happens, there are so many open opportunities for you to complete thoughts, to complement ideas, to even generate new ideas. The unfinished nature that the pencil provides to your externalizations, to your actual sketching process, is invaluable.

Imitation

For years, the industry has felt this urge to create a new mouse or come out with a new keyboard that makes it easier for a person to type, or makes it easier for someone to click around or move their hands around a mouse pad. That makes it easier to input information into computers. But what we're starting to see recently is the industry actually moving toward an imitation of the pencil—more stylus coming out that look like pencils.

They actually just came out with one that looks like a wood pencil. It's actually made up of wood. And just like the pencil is evolving into this tech product, paper is also evolving. New tablets are trying to imitate the whole paper feel. Some inventors are actually thinking about flexible prototypes, ones you can actually bend, and mobile applications that you can download, to turn any tablet into a notebook. All interesting advancements.

Natural

Software relies on a computer's capacity to execute a set of commands. Software packages are programmed to respond a certain way, to certain prompts that you, as a user, execute.

Well, the pencil is an extension of your own hand. So, in my opinion, and based on my experience, I do feel a lot more control when I am holding a pencil than when I am just prompting software to do something. It just feels like my mental hardware is working more, and it feels like a paintbrush.

When I first learned how to write calligraphy, I remember feeling this sense of magic around what I was learning. I was learning how to make other people understand my thoughts. I remember feeling that I

needed to improve this handwriting so that other people could better understand what I was thinking.

Nowadays, the emphasis on calligraphy has definitely decreased. People are not using handwriting as much. With digital signatures, and keyboards, and tablets that have input keyboards in them, on their screens, it feels like you're missing some of the sensorial experience of putting your words out there.

Also, as a writer, all of my first manuscripts are always exactly that—they're manuscripts. They're written by hand. That's when I start working on the computer, only after I've put down my ideas on paper, writing them with my hand.

In my everyday life, I like to carry around a sketchbook wherever I go. It doesn't really matter if I'm going to school, or I'm going to work, or to my office, it has to be there. It just feels like if I didn't wear socks or something—it's a part of who I am. The reason why that is is I've had so many cases where carrying around that sketchbook has saved me from losing an idea, which in my case is devastating.

If you are a writer, a designer, a creator, an entrepreneur, no matter what you are, your ideas will be everything to you. Your ideas are what keeps you going every single day. They are what makes your work make sense. The pencil allows that to happen.

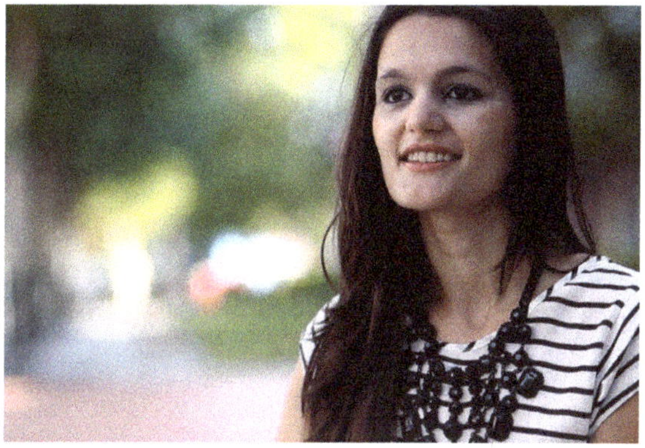

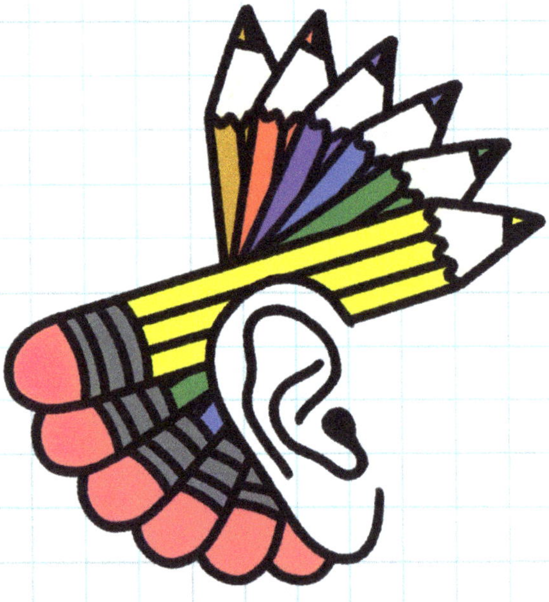

Ideas

Reshaping the Pencil

53 Pencils

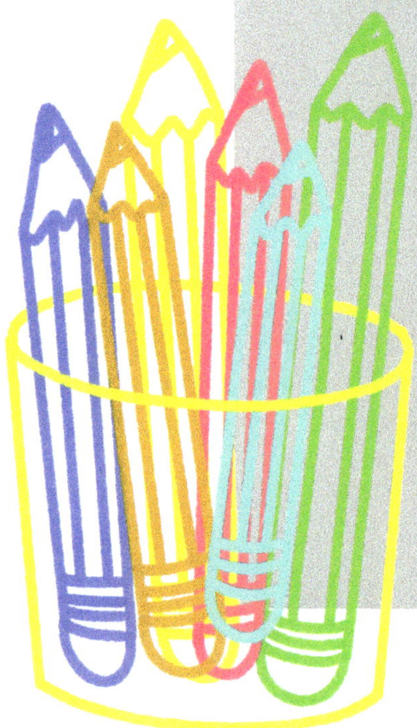

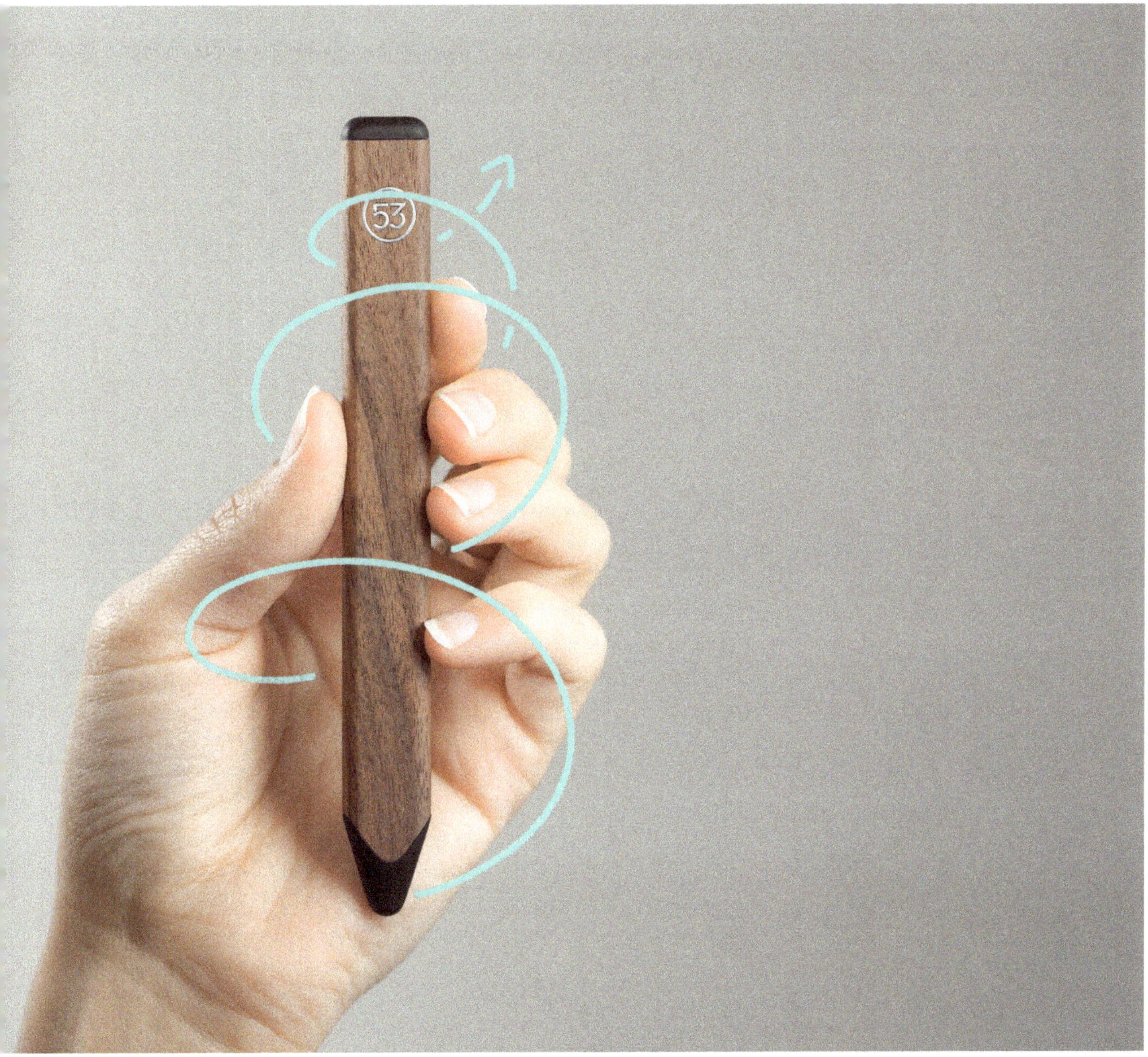

53

Over the years, we worked together at a large company and just started realizing that every time we started a new project, it began with paper and pencil. Like, regular paper and pencil. We just thought it was strange. We have invented how people game with Xbox 360, or how people listen to music, or how people use productivity tools, like Microsoft Office, but when we needed to create new projects, we would start with the good ole paper and pencil. It really opened up an entirely different perspective on what it means to make products, what it means to be creative in the digital age.

Fifty-three centimeters is the length of the average arm's reach, and that is the space between head, heart, and blank canvas. That is where creation happens. Coming from an industrial design perspective, where ergonomics and form matter so greatly, you start observing how a lot of people keep all of their most important essential important tools within arm's reach. That's why desks are about eighteen to twenty-one inches deep. That's about fifty-three centimeters.

Look at it across different cultures, across different disciplines—everyone has their sort of working zone where all important tools fall within arm's reach. It's a huge focusing call. Because if you want to play in that space, you can't overload it. You need tools that age well, that are versatile, that are well designed and well built. Because it's a precious space. Around it, we know the world of technology is always going to change. But the human need to be in that space and stay in that space is always going to remain the same.

Contributions

I had a chance to talk with the Faber Castell family, the inventors of the original pencil. I think the first pencil hit the scene in 1600-something. That family has devoted its life to making some of the best writing implements. And the way they have done this is by shaping and crafting pencils in different sizes for different hand sizes, from children to adults and professional artists.

When you look at the pencil as a tool, it's the versatility of it. With little customization, you can cater it to such a broad variety of uses. A child's hand can grasp it, an artist can master it. Everything in-between is possible with a pencil. For me, personally, it's always been an opportunity to embrace the free-form. There are hundreds of years of heritage that point to that story.

Wants for the Pencil

There are some really key things about the pencil as a tool and its advantages over any other tool. One, you can write really fine with it. The moment you tilt it on its side, you can shade. Based on sharpening, you can get different looks. It can be precise. It can be loose. When you really start to look at the quality of the line in a pencil, it goes from precise to loose, from thin to shading. Within those confines, you can do everything from a production rendered floorplan to a portrait that is gestural and free flowing. There are few tools that have that broadness of creative and expressive latitude. So, that's something to aspire to.

Limited in its Capacity

We are in an exciting moment in time when technology has entered the mainstream consciousness, meaning cell phones are within arm's reach. Tablets are there. Technology has become so powerful and integrated into people's lives that its "every day." Now we have some catching up.

Technology has become so powerful that we don't know what to do with it. I'll give you a few examples. An iPhone today is a thousand times more powerful than a computer in the late 90s. Today, everyone has one in their pocket. Similarly with tablets. Those touch displays are incredibly performant, but we don't quite even know how to develop user interfaces for it.

When you start introducing a tool like a pencil on

top of that, something that is not about just touch, but something that engages the entire hand and allows you to work with both hands where you can have the non-dominant hand control the interface, zoom into the page. You can use a pencil to sketch in more detailed ways. An entire new world opens up where the display and interface actually disappear because you are thinking with your hands.

Give it a Try

I can tell you what we hope for, and what I hope for, which is that the pencil becomes an invitation to explore your creativity, your expressiveness. That is something, up until this point, that technology has not necessarily done. We've gotten obsessed with typing and built pocket typewriters with cell phones, people tapping away.

I believe the pencil is an invitation. This is an invitation to give your creativity a try. That's the mystique of the pencil. Give creativity and creation a try. That's a fundamentally good thing. And you can do it with the physical paper and pencil. You can do it with our tools—the digital paper and pencil.

The thing that matters is that people give their creativity a try. That's it. That's what really matters. Because most people surprise themselves. Most people who stick to it, it becomes infectious. I want to live in a world where people give their creativity a try, where there are more beautiful ideas, and there is more creation. And if our pencil contributes to that, then we did something valuable. And I will be happy about that. But there is this long road ahead.

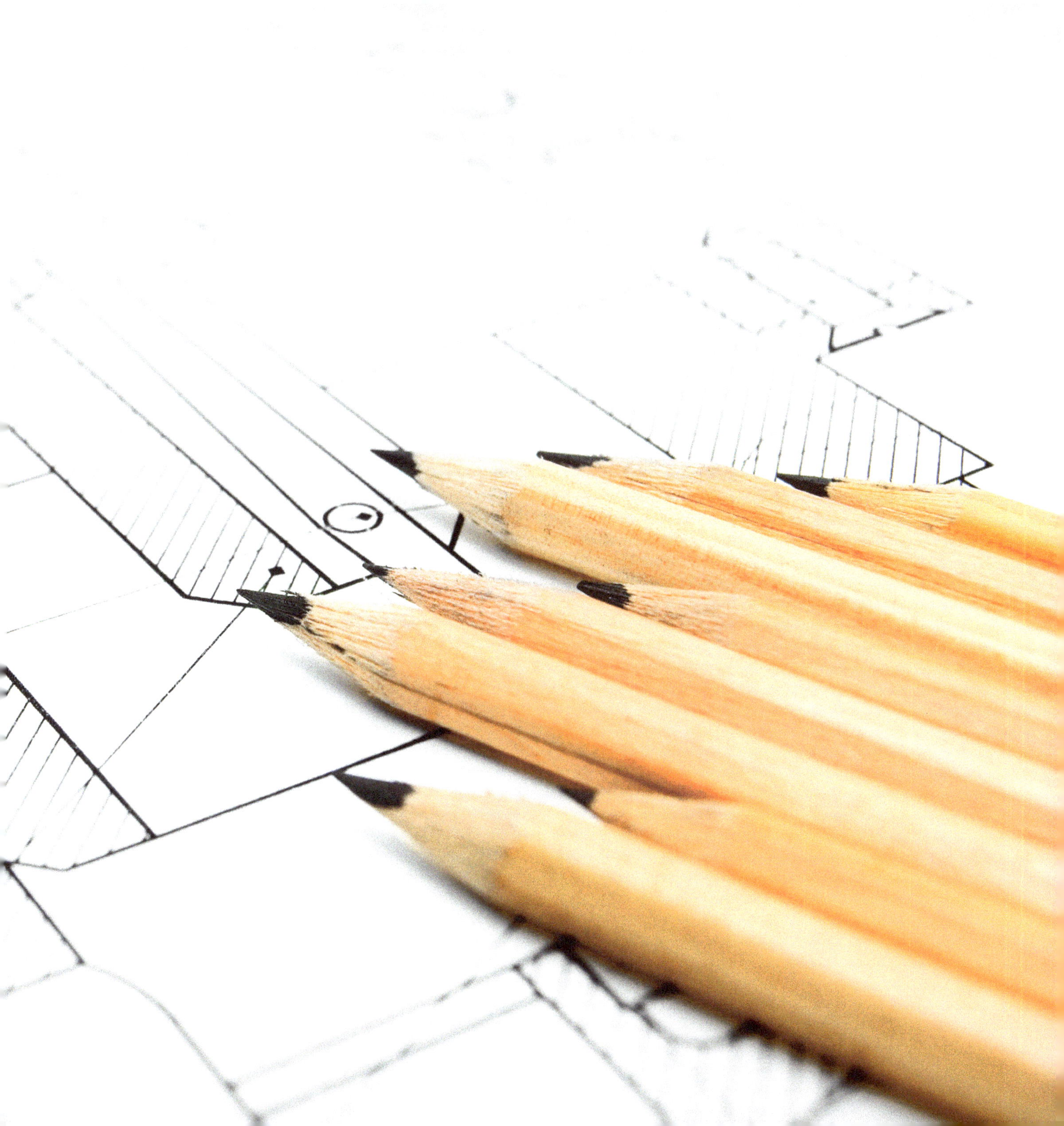

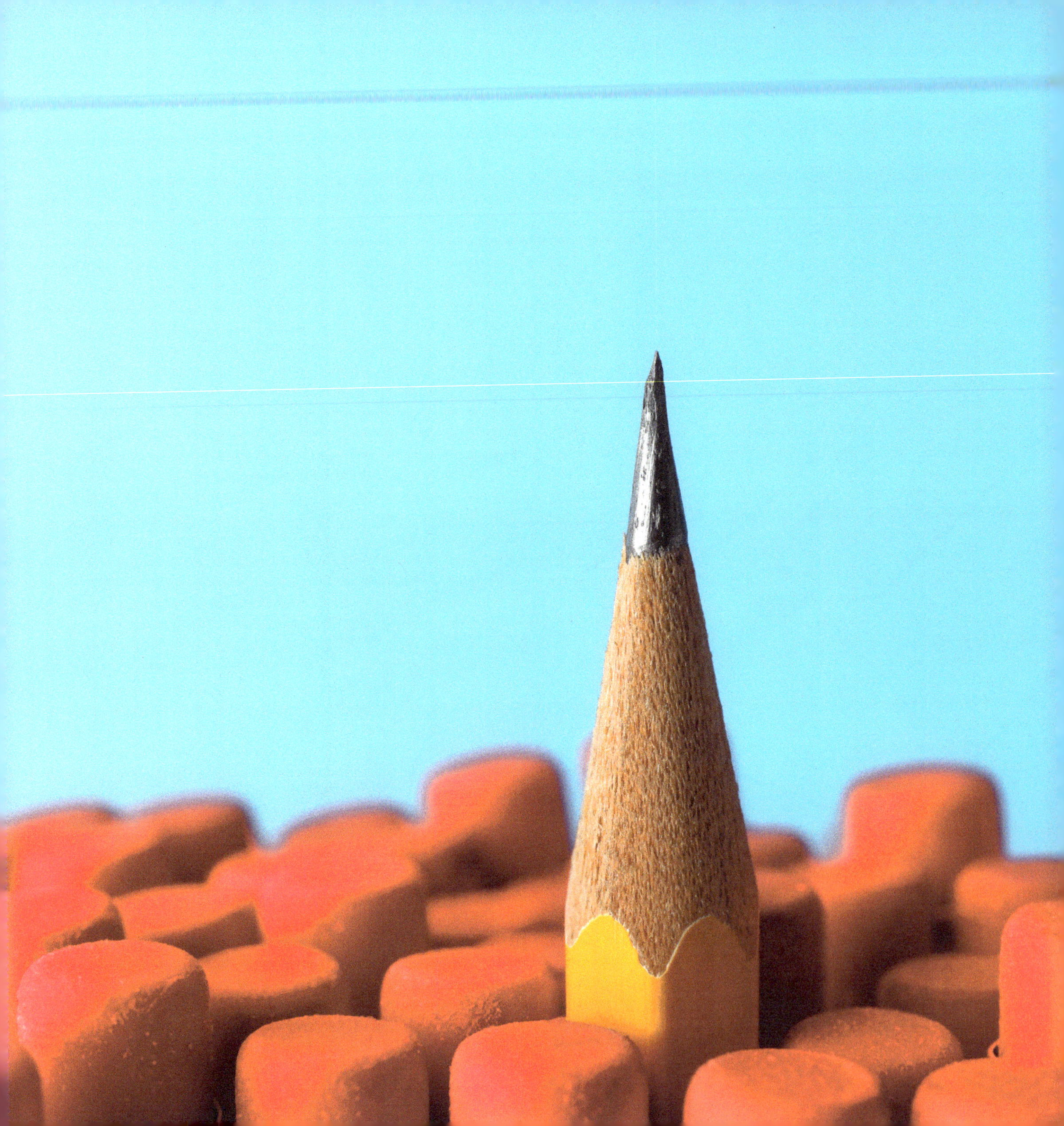

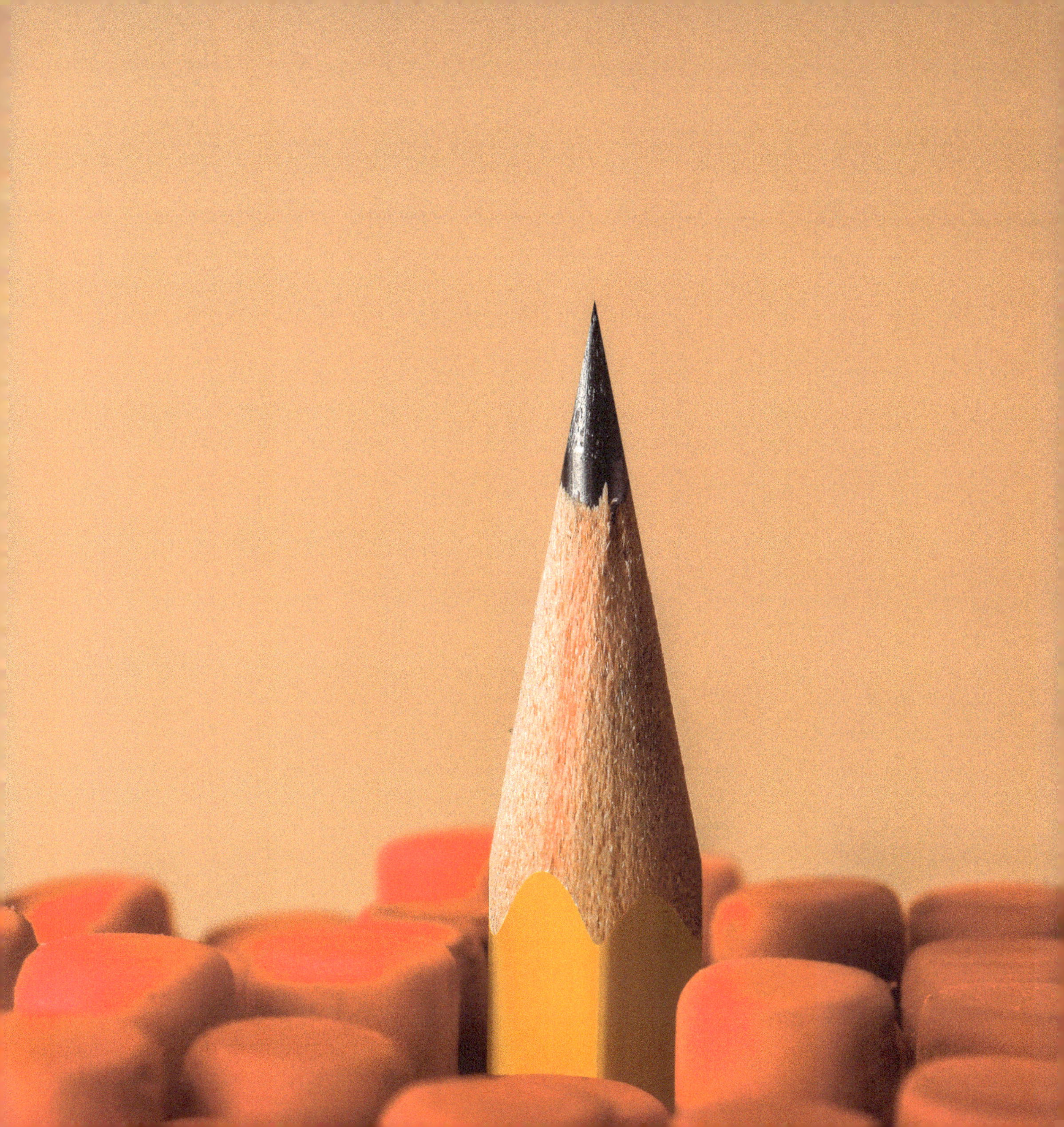

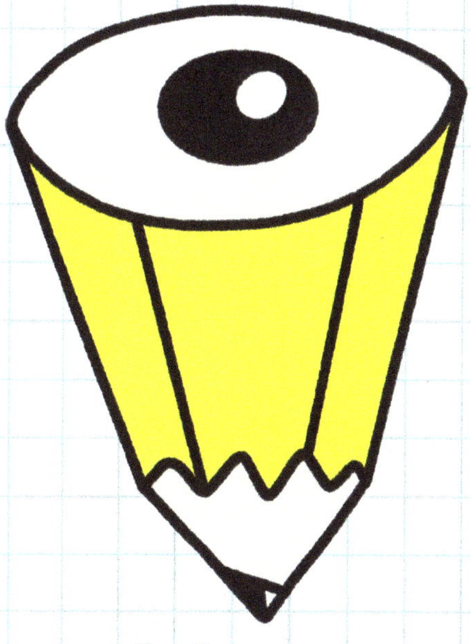

Ideas

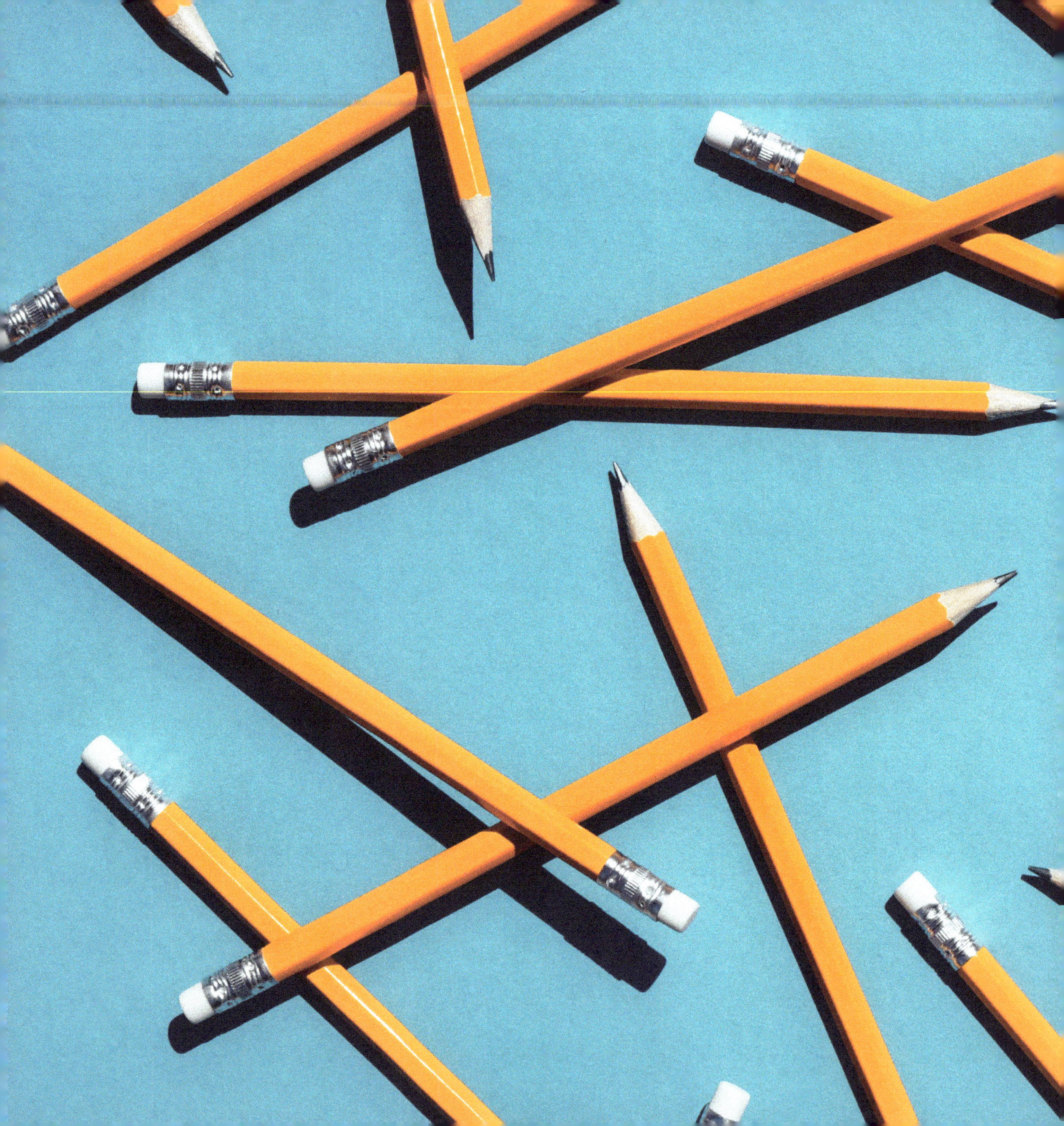

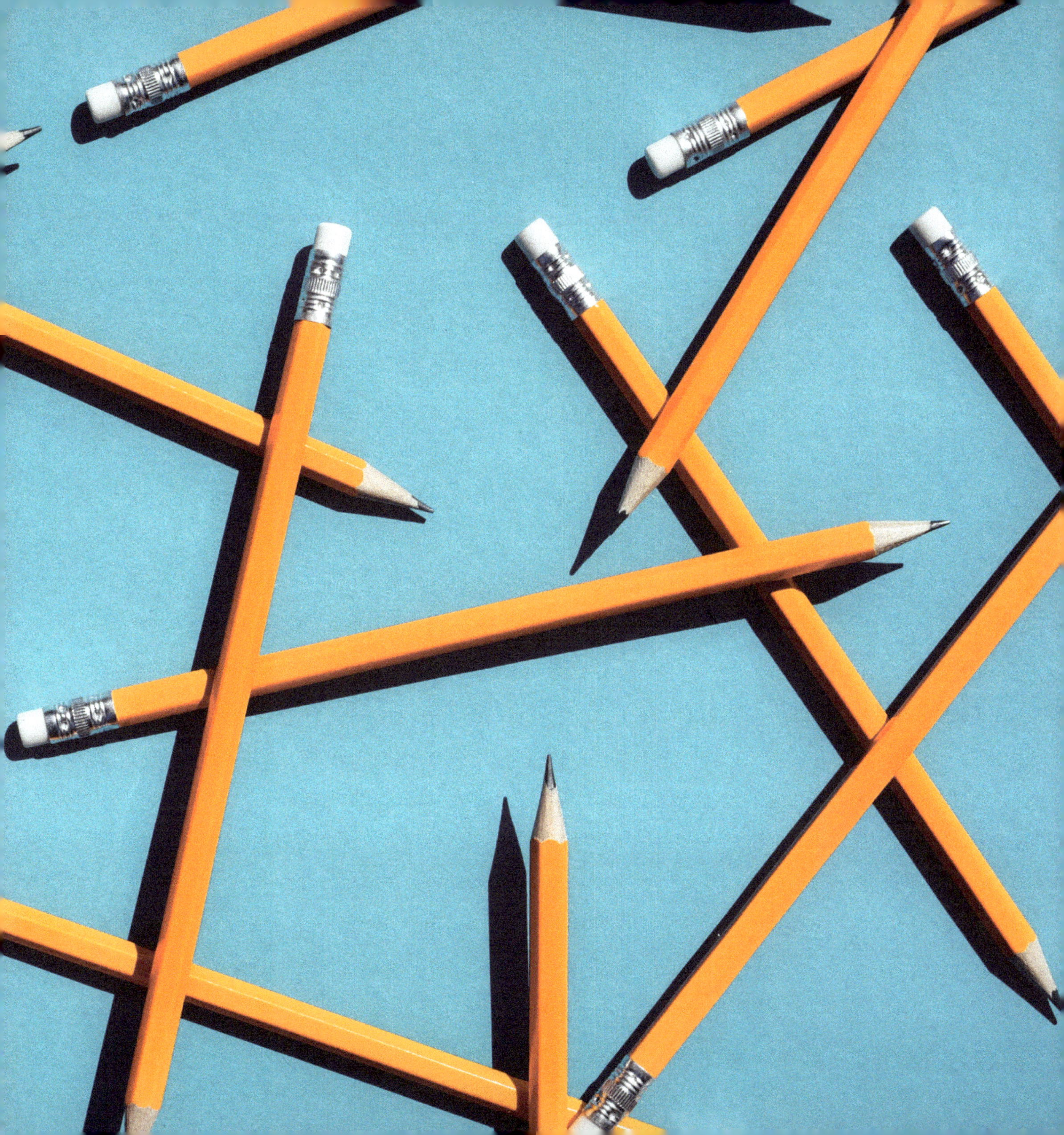

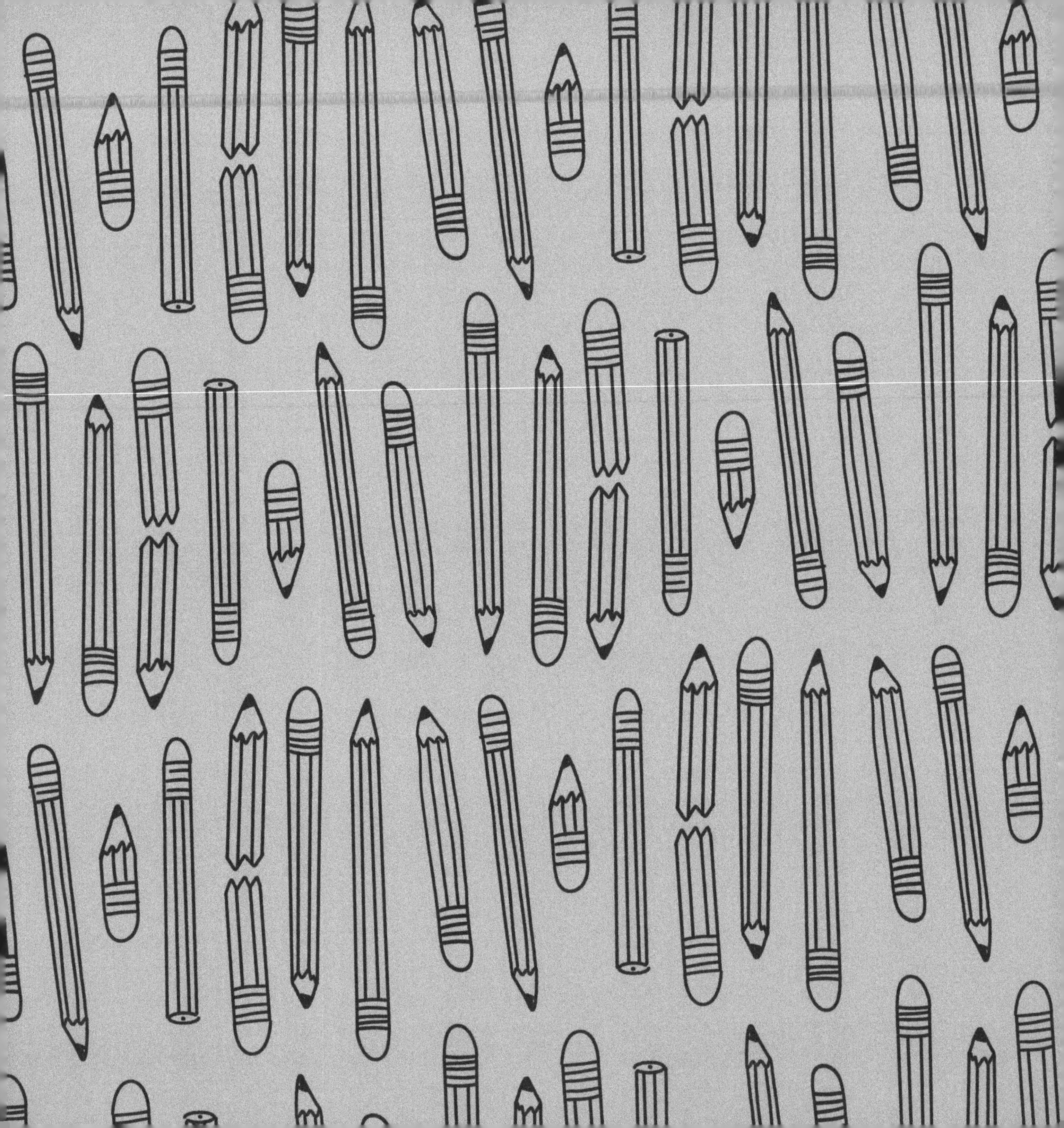

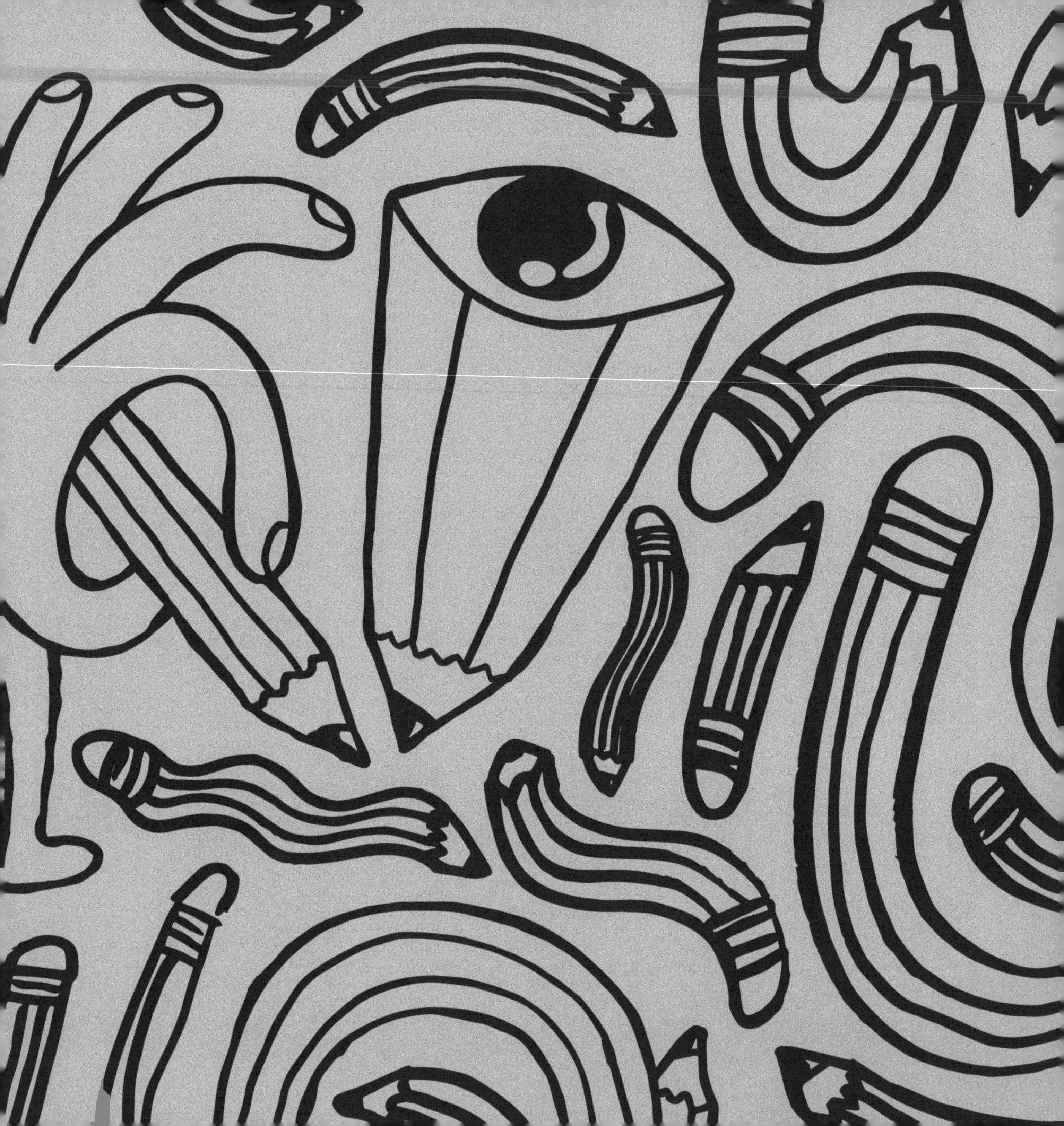

www.ingramcontent.com/pod-product-compliance
Ingram Content Group UK Ltd.
Pitfield, Milton Keynes, MK11 3LW, UK
UKHW060121010826
14089UKWH00006B/93

9 798218 260798